I0622515

13

One Woman's Sacred
Journey to Discovering Her
Greatest Power

NIKÓL ROGERS

**13: One Woman's Sacred Journey
to Discovering Her Greatest Power**

© 2023, Nikol Rogers. All rights reserved.

Published by ZenRed, Eatontown, NJ

979-8-9851630-0-1 (paperback)
979-8-9851630-1-8 (eBook)
Library of Congress Control Number: 2023901125

nikolrogers.com

Credits:
Mandala and interior geometry designs by Emily Pollio.
Author Headshot: Caitlin Cannon Photography.

"Washing the Elephant" from The Last Skin by Barbara Ras,
copyright © 2010 by Barbara Ras. Used by permission of
Penguin Books, an imprint of Penguin Publishing Group, a
division of Random House LLC. All rights reserved.

Rumi translations by Colman Barks.
Hafiz translations by Daniel Ladinsky.

Without limiting the rights under copyright reserved above, no part of this publication may be reproduced, stored in or introduced into a retrieval system, or transmitted in any form or by any means (electronic, mechanical, photocopying, recording or otherwise whether now or hereafter known), without the prior written permission of both the copyright owner and the above publisher of this book, except by a reviewer who wishes to quote brief passages in connection with a review written for insertion in a magazine, newspaper, broadcast, website, blog or other outlet in conformity with United States and International Fair Use or comparable guidelines to such copyright exceptions.

The author of this book does not dispense medical advice or prescribe the use of any technique as a form of treatment for physical or medical problems without the advice of a physician, either directly or indirectly. The intent of the author is only to offer information of a general nature to help you in your quest for emotional and spiritual well-being. In the event you use any of the information in this book for yourself, which is your constitutional right, the author and the publisher assume no responsibility for your actions.

Publication managed by AuthorImprints.com

"As inspiring as it is vulnerable, each chapter is a window into Nikol's full embrace of life—come betrayal, divorce or regrets, and ultimately, a return to love. At the end of this Qi-packed memoir, you too may be inspired to hold a furry tarantula in your hands!"
 — **Daisy Lee,** Founder, Radiant Lotus Qigong

"Nikol takes us through the sacred manifestation of a far deeper love women are desperately hungry for today. If you are a woman looking for love, go grab this book now!"
 — **Nicole Moore,** Celebrity Love Coach/TV Host

"This is an extraordinary book, rich in content and feeling, with a generous share of revelations in the power of saying 'yes' to all that is..."
 — **J. Hojin Kimmel Sensei,** Abbot of Zen
    Center of NYC, Fire Lotus Temple

"A masterpiece of truth, bridging the terrestrial to the celestial, this book is a guide for anyone that feels as though they are lost in an abyss of darkness with no way out."
 — **Alice Inoue,** Life Expert, Indie Excellence Award-
    Winning Author and Founder of Happiness U

"Nikol shows us that when we surrender the life we imagined....we are supported and a life beyond our wildest dreams is waiting."
 — **Amanda Carpenter,** Transformational Leadership
    Consultant and Heartmath Certified Coach

In this enthralling "year-in-the-life" tale, Nikol Rogers fearlessly bares her heart, her soul, her shame as every vestige of self-worth is stripped away and burned to the ground."
 — **Jeff Rubin,** Director of Unconditional Healing
    and Shambhala Buddhist Teacher

"For those of us who have ever been faced with a life crisis that consumes our best-made plans (and then spits them out), this read will scratch the itch for inspiration, joy and love."

— **Denise Braun-Stargazer, MA,** Shaman, Spiritual Therapist, Intuitive Guide

"Rogers' insightful book walks you step-by-step through the Messy Middle of true transformation with curiosity, ease and grace."

— **Samantha Bennett,** Creativity-Productivity Specialist, Bestselling Author of *Start Right Where You Are and Get It Done.*

"It takes great courage to keep our hearts open through deep pain and loss, and even more courage to lay our heart bare and let ourselves be fully seen by the world."

— **Clara Moisello,** PhD, Nonviolent Communication Trainer, Body Positive Wellness Guide

"Nikol's vulnerability, wisdom and insight will help you to successfully navigate the twists and turns of your human experience and to ignite the infinite spirit and unlimited potential that's within you!"

— **Mark Romero,** Renowned Sound Healer and Thought Leader

"...one can't help but feel more empowered, stronger and with a better sense of clarity/strategy to begin their own transformation."

— **Dr. Rodrigo Imana,** Owner of the Amayu Institute, NUCCA Practitioner

"Now is the season to know that everything you do is sacred."

                                                —*Hafiz*

TABLE OF CONTENTS

INTRODUCTION

How This Book Works

WELCOME INTO THE EXPERIENCE OF 13. I'm so grateful you are here, and to begin this intimate conversation together. Let me begin by defining what 13 is.

13 is that life moment that takes you out. It's deep devastation in the face of your broken heart and the loss you feel. It flips your world in a moment and leaves you gasping for breath, and places you at a crossroads of making big decisions. And yet in this insanity, it is also a moment of discovering your greatest power and finally experiencing the deep love your being has been yearning for. Because when you are in the experience of 13, you have the ability and newfound courage to step in a different direction when the road forks.

It becomes the moment to transform your life. What hasn't been working and the pattern of disappointment now can melt away, whereas before you may have felt terrified, powerless, and convinced you would be stuck forever.

13 is the sacred invitation, the auspicious calling to your heart to finally have the life you have always desired. The experience of 13 is deeply feminine, a co-creation with the Earth and Universe, and holds you as you take one precious step at a time. 13 is the container where you finally say, "I

want to break the pattern of destruction. I want a say in my life, and I want to experience real love."

It turns out that numbers actually play an enormous role in the direction of our lives and the time we spend here. They correlate to our journey towards love and belonging and send us messages. But we need to be spiritually awake to hear, see, and act on them.

We know the number 13 to be traditionally viewed as an unlucky number, but for me, it turned out to be the most transformative number of my life.

This book is a story about the year my life went up in flames, burning to ash all of who I thought I was. I had spent decades carefully crafting my career, marriage, persona, and friendships. But as I watched the life I had built disappear into smoke, I finally heard the call and stepped into the experience of 13.

This one year changed the course of my life, lining up in a divine pattern, one that led me to discover my greatest power. And it began with a devastating event that then whirled into a raging storm and taught me how to create a whole new beginning.

And this transformation spanned over 13 months.

This book is divided into 3 sections, 3 being the number of spiritual union. Each section will begin with a sacred number. I'll explain each number's significance throughout human history and then dive into the actual events of my story. The first section is what led to 2013, the second includes the actual events of 2013, and the third is what happened after.

I have changed all the names in this book to protect each individual as this is a personal account. The teachers and spiritual centers have also been protected to keep their privacy.

Give yourself time as you experience the book. You may find you need to journal or reflect after a certain chapter. There may be a rush of tears or surges of laughter. All is normal, and all is welcome. There is no rush, just what feels right for you, your perfect timing.

May this book open you to your greatest power and be a beacon of hope.

You are not alone. Enter into the experience of 13 knowing you are now supported. There's a reason you picked up this book. You are already following the sacred cues, which you will see within the geometrical blueprint of each page.

Just by reading, a transformation is occurring.

Now the magic and your alchemy begins.

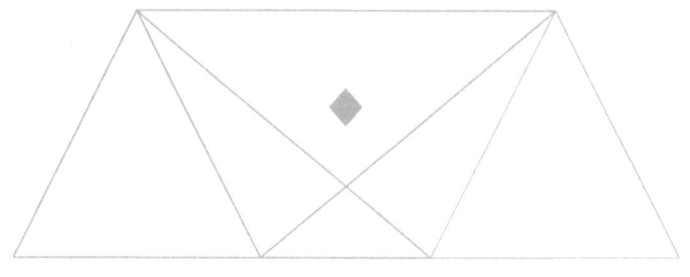

THE NUMBER 13

Is the Number 13 Lucky or Unlucky?

THERE IS A TON of historical conflict around this question. The number is so feared, it has its own phobia, Triskaideka-phobia. This fear is so prevalent, it inspired twelve slasher films and a TV series about a serial killer beyond the grave who strikes on Friday the 13th.

Scholars trace the origins of this fear back to two unlucky guests: the Norse god Loki and Judas, who both arrived to supper as the 13th to 12 already happily dining. Judas betrayed Jesus at the Last Supper, and Loki's appearance in Valhalla is said to have disturbed the balance of the 12 gods already in attendance and began a reign of evil and turmoil.

Many high-rise buildings do not have a 13th floor, and the vast majority of hotels, hospitals and airports avoid using the number for rooms and gates as well in the United States. Superstition says the number 13 brings bad luck.

But this is not the full picture.

In angelic number readings, 13 means angels are with you. When you receive this number in a reading, it's an invitation to stay positive and give any fears or doubts to the angels so that they can heal and transmute your pain.

In many cultures, 13 was known as a sacred and divinely feminine number since there are 13 moons/lunar cycles each year, not 12, and women are uniquely tied into the moon cycles. In many traditions of astrology, 13 is the luckiest number you can get, one representing your divine connection to the Universe, the goddess, and your intuitive side.

In Aztec culture, the sacred divinatory calendar was set up through 13-day cycles and conceived of time through "Aztec centuries" which were 4 periods of 13 years. For them, this unit symbolized the end of a cycle and established balance.

In the same vein, the Celtic calendar followed the rhythm of the moon and was made up of 13 months, each consisting of 28 days. These 13 months were the result of balance and harmony.

Tarot may be the most famous, and here was the reading I received months before starting to write this book. I felt it encapsulated perfectly what actually occurred for me in 2013. This reading felt like a nudge from the universe. It was no accident this reading came as I was planning to sit down and finally put this story on paper so you could read it. Because 2013 was the year that everything in my life that was not supporting me went up in a ball of smoke. It was divine timing.

> *"In traditional tarot, this is the Death card, which genuinely means life transformation in terms of death and rebirth cycles. The number 13 is showing to let you know it's time to transform whatever (or whomever) in your life is not supporting you. And to remind you that you have incredibly powerful divine beings on your side. If there are people*

in your life who don't see you, aren't respectful, or are overly critical and you feel yourself shut down around their negativity - now is the time to let those relationships go. When you release toxic or negative people from your life- or learn to draw solid boundaries with them if you can't completely remove them- you bring in new energy for yourself that is no longer defensive, draining, or angry. You will soon (or already are) experiencing much-needed breakthroughs in relationships where you've been feeling stuck, upset, or challenged. This transformative time is important to your divine mission. In living the energy of 13, you will be tapping into ancient forces and divine power for the betterment of all your relationships."

– Aurora Starr, Numerologist.

So, what is this number really? Lucky or unlucky? Death or life?

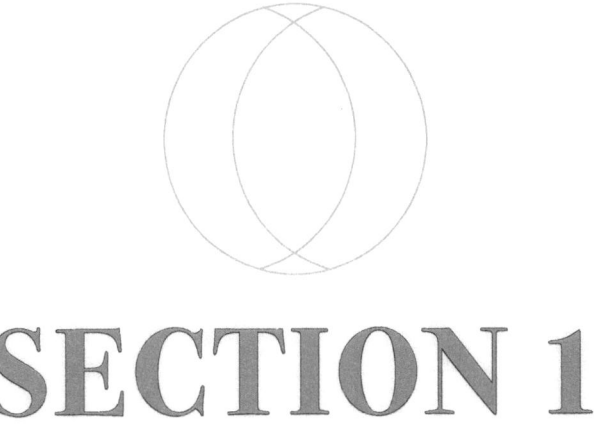

SECTION 1

12

(13 Tales in 2012)

"They developed a charming persona, a mask they created with infinite care—a mask that, as adults, may be at once their greatest blessing and greatest curse. Outwardly they may be brilliantly successful, but inwardly empty. They dream they are actors, the spotlight is on them, but they cannot remember what play they are in, let alone what their lines are."

— Marion Woodman

SHOPPING CART

MY SHOPPING CART IS FULL. I've never bought this much stuff in my life.

Every aisle seems to demand, "buy me!"

Tomorrow, after weeks of living by myself while in rehearsal for a Christmas show, I will finally have the guest I want in the cast apartment I'm staying in.

My husband of 14 years.

So I grab two of everything. Double.

I grab candles that smell nice, a large spaghetti squash, and a huge bag of pistachios. He likes those. I want to have everything he could possibly need there.

When I get to the cashier, I almost fall over. I've never spent this much. But as the bagger puts everything into paper, all I can think is, *do I have enough?*

Tomorrow is Thanksgiving and my day off as dance captain before the theater goes into tech for their big Christmas musical. The whole cast is gathering at the director's house, and it will be the first time everyone is meeting my husband. I can't wait for him to see the show.

I stumble with all my heavy bags out of the taxi into the apartment the theater has provided and take time to put everything away in my small kitchen. The fridge is bursting, and I put all kinds of treats, candles, and a huge bowl of pistachios out.

Everything looks amazing. So I go to sleep knowing that—in the morning—I'm ready.

We are finally seeing each other. This year is the most time we have spent apart in our marriage, but he will be here.

It's all going to be ok.

GINGERBREAD

I'M AT MY DIRECTOR'S HOUSE for the Thanksgiving cast party. Sitting in the main dining room, my companion at the table is one of the children in the show, Katy. Being an adolescent, she is very excited about the icing. We paired up to make a gingerbread house, as my husband didn't want to.

While putting up the thick cookie walls and picking out gumdrops, I see his blank face staring at the screen in the other room. I know he enjoys his football, but this is crazy...

Why am I putting this house together by myself?

Why isn't he socializing with anyone? The whole cast has been waiting weeks to meet him, and many have tried to engage him in conversation with no luck.

And why did he eat so many pistachios before coming to this potluck Thanksgiving? I had greeted him with such glee and watched him eat nut after nut, creating a stack of shells—all piled up on the coffee table—before coming to Thanksgiving dinner.

He seemed to stare in shock at all the food I bought for our time together. And his suitcase remained closed and propped against the wall. He didn't even unpack his toothbrush.

I finish the gingerbread house. Katy is beaming, but I'm feeling really strange. I look over at my husband's face. He's still watching the football game, so I get up and cross to the TV room.

"Do you want to go?" I ask.

SHOELACE

"WE NEED TO TALK."

I see his suitcase behind him, the pile of shells next to him, and his eyes darting around.

"I don't think I love you anymore."

"I don't think I want to be married anymore."

"I don't think I want to have children."

Hole opening up.

"I started seeing a therapist weeks ago."

Chest starting to burn.

"I brought condoms because I didn't want to chance it."

I'm now on fire, rising from the couch. Our voices raise. I can't feel my feet.

Back and forth we yell, until he is slamming his hand against the wall admitting he is in love with someone else.

I knew it. I knew it. I felt it when I went to see him in the musical he was starring in this summer. I felt it when I met her and saw them on stage together.

And he kneels before me and asks me with complete honesty, "When was the last time I said I love you and meant it?"

Is he REALLY asking me this? Does he not know?

Dear GOD... did I know?

And I'm yelling.

I'm screaming.

How long has he been acting?

The walls shake with our voices, and then he grabs his shoes and starts tightening the laces at 11 at night, with nowhere to go but the Salt Lake airport and says, "One of these days you'll make a mistake and know how it feels."

And I know it's finally time to tell him.

COUCH

JUST LIKE ME, HE KNEW. He guesses who it was, another showmance turned affair.

For a minute, Jon's face loosens and he laughs, "We both did it."

I tell him so he knows he's not alone.

I tell him so he knows I get it.

I do make mistakes. I'm not perfect.

I did it too.

I look into Jon's eyes and say out loud for the first time what I've been wanting to say all year. I wasn't in love with this other man. I thought the affair would bring me happiness, and it only brought me pain.

He never loved me how I wanted to be loved. The affair was empty. And I realized I wanted to be married to my husband. I recommitted.

For 5 minutes, the air changes in the room. Our voices are quiet, and I see an opening. I've spent the last four years trying to hide this from him, but am sharing it now to save us.

I think it's working.

And then a cloud comes over his face and the window is gone. His whole body goes rigid.

I'm yelling again. He's yelling and pounding the walls. I don't even know what time it is anymore. I feel like my whole body is on fire. I finally unloaded this secret I've been holding for four years, and it only created more harm.

We yell ourselves to exhaustion. And while he starts snoring within minutes of laying down to sleep in the bed with me, I can't take it.

"You have to sleep on the couch."

Journal Entry
11/23/12

Today I stared at the shell of a man, my husband, and did not recognize his gaunt face, his jeans loose on his legs, his sad empty eyes, and his overcoming his fear as he turned the handle and walked out of my apartment.

I was blindsided, I was humiliated, I was shamed by his selfish actions, his fear of "locking in" with children, his affair with Shannon and the news he's seeing a therapist. What happened? I knew he was scared. I saw the distance, but we made the decision together last year to get off the pill and start trying. And it was hell; my hormones were all over the place, I did acupuncture, I charted my temp, I took herbal tea… and my cycle just got longer and longer.

It was his suggestion to stop everything. He saw it was destroying me, making me obsessive, and I kept asking him to stop with negative comments about raising children. But we made the decision together. I kept reassuring him…

I didn't want to spend the summer apart. It was five weeks until I saw him for my birthday, and he was distant. We fought, had sex, and then all was right again… except for the fact that he had sex with Shannon after I left.

Of course, there is a grave irony here, but I always believed and I always said he was a better person than me. I believed he made me a better person. And he did this, this crime.

He went back to her when I was doing my next gig and was so strange and judgmental when he came to visit. We fought again. I cried, but I couldn't imagine the truth.

And then Thanksgiving… he drops the bomb he is seeing a therapist and isn't sure whether he wants to be in this marriage anymore. Said I love him too much, that I deserve a man who will have kids with me… funny, he had promised me that man was him. Told me he had a panic attack when I was home before the Christmas musical because he thought I was pregnant. Oh, and he's fallen in love with Shannon. What??

Where did he go? What crazy, selfish spiral did he go on? Turning 40, getting skinny, new haircut, having sex with a girl in her 20s. My husband, the cliche. My husband, the joke. And me? Completely dumbfounded, heartbroken, smashed to a pulp. I have never had such feelings of hate towards him, his fear, his cowardice.

So I told him about Dan. I never thought the day would come... and he laughed.

I couldn't have him here, unable to fight, unable to answer a simple question, "What do you want?"

I barely slept, made him sleep on the couch, and how I hoped I would wake to him begging for me, for my love. Instead I was met with defeat and dead stares. His love for me... gone. I honestly didn't think it was possible.

Everything I've been through, and my constant, my foundation, was always my feelings for him.

For the first time, I saw a possibility I was going to get a divorce and have to start over... at 37.

He made a decision for both of us, but this is NOT what I want. He shut me out. He fucked me over and thinks we will never recover.

He may be right.

I called Shannon today—after getting the number off my husband's phone—and confronted her. I was shaking, but it felt so good. I told her never to call or text my husband again. She's a fucking homewrecker, and I will tell people. She better hope we never meet.

So now... what? My husband had to go home, away from me. He's going back to therapy, and I'm back home in NYC in 3 weeks. I don't know what to do with all the anger.

THIS IS NOT WHAT I WANT.

This is not the life I've built.

All that history

All that love and he can't find it.

And all because I want
to have a family with him
and love him.

What an asshole.

BLACK FRIDAY

I HAVE TO GO TO WORK.

I have a 10-hour rehearsal, and I have to lie to everyone and say my husband's grandmother is sick to explain his abrupt departure.

I'm not going to tell them my husband wants to leave me and is in love with another woman. I'm not going to tell them I didn't sleep last night. I've been lying to everyone for so long, I guess another three weeks won't make a difference.

I have to go to work, so I roll out my yoga mat to do my warm-up before heading to the theater.

And as I close my eyes for a moment to catch my breath, a voice comes up very clear within, *"You need meditation."*

Yea… considering it looks like I'm about to lose everything, that would probably be helpful.

MANTRA

YOGA MAT ROLLED OUT for warm-up again. Have to get ready for work after another sleepless night.

Maybe I'll try meditating, but have no idea how to start or what to do.

I do a quick search for meditations to ease stress and find the Sa Ta Na Ma meditation.

The sounds are familiar from my many years in yoga class, and I now learn there are meanings to the words. I immediately start to weep when I read them.

Sa – birth, cosmos

Ta – life

Na – death, transformation

Ma – rebirth

I start to join my thumb to my first finger, then second, then third, and pinky as I say each one. Repeat again. Repeat again, letting the rhythm of the mantra express through my hands.

Repeat again over and over, out loud and then silently as I close my eyes.

Sa Ta Na Ma.

Sa Ta Na Ma.

Sa Ta Na Ma.

Rolling through me, my fingertips joining in rhythm, almost automatically.

Tears are falling, but I feel some strength to face the day.

OPENING NIGHT

NOTHING. NOT A SINGLE CARD OR GIFT. For the first time in our 18 years of being together, I have nothing from my husband.

I have shoeboxes back at home full of beautiful cards from him, sometimes two for a special show, all arriving just in time to celebrate one of the most sacred days in theater, Opening Night.

But not tonight.

The dressing room is packed with cards, flowers, high energy, and I'm breathing as slowly as I can when I see no mail at my place.

As no one here knows what is really going on, I feel like I'm strangled. I feel so alone.

And then I decide, "Fuck him." I'm going to enjoy this night without him.

Without him.

The audience erupts with a standing ovation, and I put on a new dress and go to the Opening Night party.

And I drink.

And I drink.

And I decide to text Dan. He responds quickly and celebrates with me. I know I said it was over, but this feels good.

He cares, at least, when his girlfriend isn't around.

Texting turns to sexting, to full on FaceTime once I got home, then phone sex, except I can't climax. I'm rubbing and rubbing. Dan is done and waiting for me. "Talk dirty to me," I plead... anything. I hold the phone down so all he sees is my mound because my face has become so constricted and tense.

I finally climax and say lackluster words of good night. I thought I would feel better.

I then wash my face, crawl into bed and can't stop crying.

I can't believe I just did it again...

It wasn't Dan's face I wanted to see tonight.

So much burning in my chest.

Journal Entry
12/13/12

Today was probably the worst day since Thanksgiving. I woke up after a dream of missing a train that my dream book said means "a separation is unavoidable" and I've lost an opportunity... I panicked. I felt so deeply it was over.

How did it go from 0 to 60 so fast? How can he cause me so much pain, hear me bawling, and still be dead inside??

I went to see the movie Silver Linings Playbook today and it was the biggest mistake. Way too close to home and Bradley Cooper's wife's name was Nikki. Bradley Cooper ended up picking the younger Jennifer Lawrence and falling in love with her. I couldn't stop crying because all I remember is my husband saying what a great movie it was... and I sobbed in the bathroom stall after. I couldn't stop myself coming out and called my husband, leaving a message saying what a rough day I was having. He did call me back once I was back in my apartment and it was the greatest hits,

"I'm sorry"

"We can't hash this out over the phone."

"We will work it out once you get back."

Is he deaf? He offers nothing to my plea, "I need reassurance. What is going to change once I'm in front of you?"

He's not fighting for me. And instead I hear him say, "relax. Calm down."

I told him this timeline, this refusing to engage is his doing, not what I want. NONE of this is what I want, and I keep hoping my vulnerability will inspire the man I knew... and it doesn't. I keep making myself vulnerable... for what??

I finally said, "don't worry. I won't call again, no matter how upset I am. See you Sunday." and hung up. And he has the fucking nerve to text me, "please call your mom. You'll feel better once you talk to someone."

My reply?

FUCK YOU.

TARANTULA

THE THEATER HOLDS A HOLIDAY PARTY for us, and has an animal interaction company set up down in our main rehearsal hall. We have many kids in the cast, so they are all thrilled.

I put on my red top, holiday earrings, and go.

The last conversation with my husband still ringing in my ears, I enter the room.

I immediately hear the gleeful cries of our younger cast mates, and see giant tortoises slowly crawling on the floor. I feel a smile coming, and make my way around to the back of the room where my friend Tina has a giant yellow boa constrictor wrapped around her. She's laughing and the other dancers are all gathered around to see her handling this massive snake when out of nowhere, one of the animal handlers pops a tarantula on Tina's head.

I completely freeze.

Every hair on my body has gone into high alert as I look over behind Tina and see a table with 4 Tarantulas sitting as if they were flower arrangements.

I see myself standing in the basement of my youth, terrified of the massive black spiders who took up residence in every dark window, torturing me.

And then the trainer looks at me and asks, "you want to hold the spider?"

My decades of arachnophobia are screaming, "NO!", and then a completely new thought comes into my head.

I had always thought my biggest fear was spiders, but here I was living my biggest fear… losing my marriage and ability to have the family I deeply desired. I was living it, and somehow was still breathing each day, so maybe I could hold a spider.

I hold out my hand, and the trainer places the tarantula in my palm. It starts to scurry, and I suddenly realize I need to calm down so it won't freak out so much. I start to breathe deeper and the tarantula stops moving and just stands frozen in the center of my hand. I look down and see its abdomen is shaking and I realize, "oh my gosh..it's just as scared as I am."

I feel a calming within and the spider seems to relax. I notice how soft the tarantula's fur is, and how lightweight.

It was nothing like I thought. My fear was nothing like I thought.

Just as I'm smiling at conquering a fear I have had for 30 years, a friend takes a picture.

Then the trainer says to me, "Want to hold a scorpion?"

Without a beat, I reply, "Sure!"

This becomes my new profile picture, and I go home, reaching for my journal to write,

Today, I held a tarantula in my hands... my greatest fear, and it was docile, just as scared as I, and soft.

Today I held a python around my arms, a scorpion in the palm of my hand, and a bearded dragon on my chest.

Today I told my mother about my husband's affair and she finally understood my anger.

Today was a beautiful day.

Journal Entry
12/18/12

I am home… if I can even call it that. The sight of my husband unhinged me, I was so overwhelmed with my love for him, it struck me silent. It was a travel day from hell from Salt Lake to NYC, and though I thought the fatigue would take the edge off, I found myself suffocating, surrounded by everything we have built and trying to make sense of his actions and hate. Here, in our home, our things, our beautiful marriage, all on display, and he's blinded by fear and a 25 year old.

I sobbed through eating food he heated up for me..he gave me a hug, held me, but I kept my arms crossed in protection. I listened to his heartbeat. It used to calm me, and I felt like a trapped and scared animal. I went into the bedroom, curled up in a tight ball against my college dresser and bawled… my home, a strange place, my husband, a strange man… and the time away felt so long. It was acute and terrible.

I sobbed while eating as he sat across from me and watched. Gather 'round and see what you have done, what you are doing.

We started talking, then anger, everything coming out. It's starting to bleed together in my sleep-deprived state. He yelled at me, "You know how to push my buttons!" Exploded the bomb on me that he shared my affair and his with his parents… more surprises, more things he was keeping from me…

DINOSAUR

I OPEN HIS CLOSET DOOR. Jon is staying at a friend's for the weekend. And I'm here alone, praying he finally wakes up from this craziness and comes back to his senses. Our couple's therapist recommended I give him some space, and I feel like I can't breathe.

But I'm doing it. I'll do anything to save our marriage.

I touch his clothes hanging there and then walk in and embrace every sleeve. Inhaling deep, I can smell him. The familiarity, all our history, and my hands grip tightly to the fabric.

After a long while, I let go, and the clothes swing back into place. I look down at the bottom of the closet to see a paper bag and pull out a toy dinosaur.

It's a small T-Rex. When you press its tongue, it makes this adorable sound. Years ago, when Jon brought it back from a toy show he was working, I felt like my ovaries lit up like the night sky when I saw it.

"Oh! We have to keep this! We can give it to our children!"

And he did keep it, and every so often, I would open his closet and press the dinosaur's tongue as a way to remind myself of this vision, of us having a child together.

I hold the dinosaur in my hands, and press the tongue to hear the noise again, only to hear silence. The battery ran out.

Who knows how long ago?

And I slump down to the floor, overcome with the fear that I will never have the family I want.

PICTURE FRAME

I'VE LOCKED MYSELF IN THE BEDROOM.

I'm not going to eat.

I didn't sleep, but all I want to do is cry.

I grab the gold and silver picture frame above our bed—the photo of us from our wedding day. It has always been my favorite photo of the two of us. We are dancing our first dance, my eyes closed as I lay my head against his chest in pure contentment. While he holds me with such confidence, he's staring upward, towards the sky.

I pull the frame into my chest and start to wail.

I don't care if the neighbors hear me.

I don't care who hears me.

This is the sound of my being broken open. Cracked wide, and purged from my throat in primal cries.

Nothing is working.

Not the magic of Christmas morning and giving him the perfect gift.

Not the hope of a New Year as the ball drops.

Not couple's therapy.

I crawled under the pull-out bed where he was sleeping in the living room, shrinking into the fetal position, refusing to come out. My husband pleaded with me. I didn't want to come out until he promised he wasn't going to leave. Until he said he loves me.

That didn't work, and I crawled out completely defeated and went to sleep in the bedroom alone, again.

I even thought about jumping out of the bathroom window or burning myself on the heat pipe.

I called his mother, his father, and even his best friend, pleading with them to help me. Help me convince him to stay. All three listened and quietly refused. I thought they were my allies. I thought they would want our marriage to last. I was losing them too.

Nothing I tried was working.

It's falling apart, and I can't stop it.

I can't stop it.

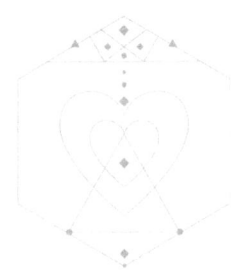

THE NUMBER 7

SEVEN MAY BE ONE of the most powerful and loved numbers we have. Significant since ancient times and across multiple cultures, 7 represents divinity and spiritual transformation. Many magicians know that when you ask someone to choose a number from 1 to 10, most will choose 7.

Why?

Well, we have the seven days of the week, and countless references in all the major religions. In the Old Testament, the world was created in six days and God rested on the seventh. The Koran speaks of seven heavens, and in Mecca, Muslim pilgrims walk around Islam's most sacred site, the Kaaba, seven times. In Hinduism, there are seven higher worlds and seven underworlds, and in Buddhism, texts speak of the newborn Buddha rising and taking seven steps, signaling his enlightenment to come.

We have the seven wonders of the world, and in Chinese culture, seven represents the combination of Yin, Yang, and the Five Elements—Metal, Wood, Water, Fire, and Earth. Confucianism regards this combination as harmony.

Yoga teaches us we have seven chakras, core energy centers in the human body. By activating and aligning them, energy flows through your body easier, creating good health.

In alchemical thought, seven is associated with self realization. When it appears in your life, it is a sign that a transformation is complete and is the best you could have wished for. But for this to happen, you need to clear the negative things in your life. They urge you to not be afraid to give up what no longer serves you. The number seven is here for you.

And in numerology, seven represents the spiritual maturity that comes after a learning cycle.

Learning, indeed. For me, that learning was an awakening, and took 7 major steps.

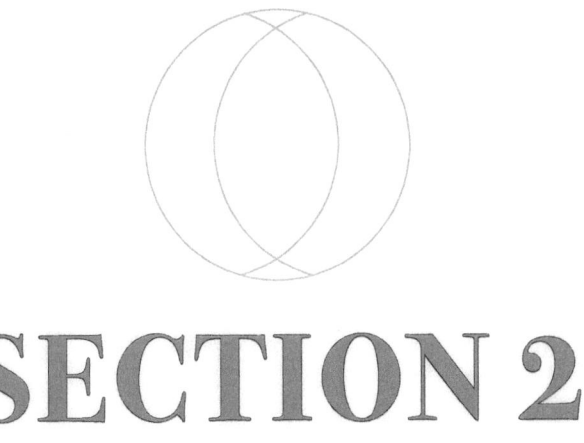

SECTION 2

THE 7 STEPS IN AWAKENING

"The fundamental question in most spiritual traditions is, who am I?"

– Tara Brach

STEP 1
SATI

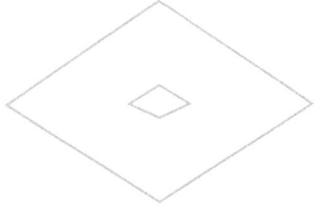

Introversion of Attention

X-RAY

I CAN'T STOP COUGHING.

I've also lost a lot of weight.

Ironically, my husband—I don't even know what to call him anymore—is concerned and encourages me to go to the doctor.

Apparently an uncontrollable cough and weight loss are not a good combo.

Couple's therapy lasted a whopping two and half weeks. We wanted completely different things. I wanted to save the marriage, and he wanted to have a third party to be witness to what he was saying.

In our final session, Jon's every answer ended with him going on about how great Shannon was and how much he loved her. Each comment caused me to curl into the fetal position in agony. I have never felt more invisible in my life. He didn't seem to see me shrink and break right beside him on the couch.

When we walked out the front entrance of the building, I told him to go home and pack his bags. As I started to take steps away from him on the street, my whole body went into panic. The sidewalk didn't make any sense, and I was going into shock.

I called my mother, shaking. "I don't know what to do!"

"Go back to the therapist," she pleaded with me.

I turned around and, thankfully, the therapist hadn't left and was actually just as shaken as I was at what she had just witnessed in the session.

She opened her door, let me sit on her couch, and three words spilled out of my mouth with the force of a torrent waterfall, "I need help."

For four years, I had wanted to talk to a therapist. For four years, I had cried in the shower after seeing Dan again and lying to my husband. For four years, I wanted to tell my mother and best friend, but was so scared they would stop loving me. For four years, I wondered how I could go see a therapist without my husband knowing.

I knew we were in trouble. I knew I was in trouble. But I was terrified to ask for help. So I just tried to control everything and put on an act that I had it all together. I drank more, jammed my earphones into my ears to drown out my mind with constant loud music, and watched as much TV as possible.

The lie literally grew in my body. I had cancerous cells removed from my cervix. Even though I was trying to do all I could to suppress it, my tissues remembered.

The lies got bigger and bigger. Shame took over my belly, and after a year and a half of trying, I was not pregnant.

And then he did it. I almost admired my husband in the moment of admitting he sought the help he needed, and also felt hope that, with couple's counseling, the marriage could be saved because we both recognized how valuable it was.

Except it didn't matter. The trust was broken. The divide had become a wall.

So, as I sat on the therapy couch by myself for the first time in my life, I finally let go and accepted what I had needed for a long time.

I needed help.

And it was there waiting for me.

I just needed to ask for it.

January filled with work, all set up months before I knew I would also be dealing with a divorce. Days after the ball dropped, I was setting up for Intermezzo with the contemporary fashion line I had a part time job with.

The owner, Adesh, looks at me as I hang all the new silk samples, and after grabbing another cough drop, I tell him.

He can't believe it.

"Let me talk to him," he offers, his big, warm eyes like a hug. I feel so grateful to be spending my days with him right now. Working for him and his beautiful clothing line have been a real source of joy over the past three years, and he has become a cross between a dear friend and father figure. I really see myself growing with his company and have gone from helping out on shows to becoming his corporate sales rep.

Apparently, the fashion world and the performing world have a lot in common. So many of my audition stories and his meetings have the same themes of showing up with our best intentions, a great product, and then getting rejected. We share our disappointments, our laughter, and the best motivation we can give each other.

His belief in my career is as high as my belief in his clothing line. Which is good, because we are both floundering, frustrated, and have hit a ceiling.

After setting up the booth and ending my day with Adesh, I find a walk-in clinic and wonder if today I'll be receiving more bad news, except this time it will be about my cough.

I'm called into a cavernous examination room where a doctor asks me what is going on and holds his cold stethoscope to my chest.

"Let's do an X-ray," he states.

A technician comes into the room, and I hear the loud whirr of the machine photographing my insides.

I watch him leave, return again with the film, and then go to the end of the room to look at it. I can't tell from his expression what he is seeing. His face is completely neutral.

Is this good or bad?

"Would you like to see?" he asks.

I walk over, expecting to see a huge black mass on the film, only to look up at a completely clear X-ray.

"Everything looks clear! You have really strong lungs. You could survive underwater for a long time," he offers.

My eyes widen at his choice of words.

And I feel the turbulent seas calm just for a moment. I honestly thought I was drowning.

Maybe not.

Maybe I do want to live.

BOOKSHELF

TODAY IS THE DAY.

I am returning to yoga class for the first time since I landed at Laguardia Airport last December and entered into the hell of my life falling apart.

I haven't been to yoga class in weeks. My whole body is screaming for it.

And since it's now clear divorce is happening, I want to feel something GOOD.

I can't remember a day when I haven't cried. Maybe today will be that day.

The clunking of the steam pipes in the studio may be the most beautiful music I've ever heard, and in shavasana, I feel myself melt into the mat, into the floor.

I even stop coughing for five minutes.

When the doors open, I pick up my mat and head for the studio store, and decide today I am going to buy a book on meditation. I hadn't forgotten the voice that arose on Black Friday. Maybe this will help.

I look at the shelf and see the categories in simple stickers along the ivory wood. Seeing "meditation" midway, I read the title and immediately grab it.

Every word is popping off the page. It's as if the author is speaking directly to me.

And I suddenly realize I've picked up a book on Tibetan Buddhism. *Wait, I thought I was looking for meditation...*

I buy the book and continue to devour it in two days, dog-earing page after page.

TEA

MY FRIEND HANDS ME two email addresses written on a small piece of paper.

One is a client of his going through a divorce right now, and the other is divorced. And they are both Buddhists.

"Maybe talking to them will help," he warmly offers before giving me a deep hug.

I reach out to both of them, and the first woman, a writer named Cathy who has been divorced for quite some time, responds right away with an invitation for tea. I accept with gratitude and head downtown to her apartment the next day.

She opens the door, taking me in with comforting eyes, and I walk into her spacious kitchen. The sun is shining through wide windows, washing the floor with a golden light. I immediately feel better being here.

"Would you like some tea?" she asks.

Holding the steaming cup with shaking hands, I sit across from her, and the floodgates open. I tell her every-thing, and I'm weeping.

She then grabs a small yellow sheet of paper and starts writing.

Handing me the paper, I look down at the top, at four words I've never heard before:

NAM MYO HORENGE KYO

She gently shares with me, "'Nam' means I devote myself. 'Myo' is the tangible and intangible, the world that I can see and not see. 'Horenge' is the lotus flower. The lotus is blooming in mud. It cleans itself, blooms and seeds at the same time. This is cause and effect. 'Kyo' means in the spirit of the Buddha."

I ask for a pen and start frantically taking notes. It feels like my whole body is coming alive. Cathy waits patiently for my pen to stop, and then continues when she sees my eyes raise with expectation, ready for what she will say next.

"Make a list every night. List out what you are grateful for. Make a list of your victories, even if all that happened that day is you did laundry."

My pen is racing as fast as it can again. I'm in complete student mode, hanging on her words and somehow knowing I need to write this all down. I don't want to miss any of it. And while I was already using a gratitude practice, I never thought to actually list out victories. I was certainly feeling like I was constantly in a state of losing right now. What if laundry could be a victory? This was a radical thought.

And then she asks, "Would you like to learn how to chant?"

I follow her to the corner of her living room where she has a small altar set up. She lights a candle and instructs me to say those four words together, over and over.

NAMMYOHORENGEKYO

I start slow and then pick up the pace, and we chant together.

I feel something loosening inside.

"You can create an altar of your own. Try chanting for the next week. Find a nice neutral focus on the wall and stay engaged. Have an intention around your desires, your aspiration, and go with an open heart. Pour out your heart as you chant."

When she sees the other yellow paper is full, she hands me another sheet and the pen, and we sit across from one another as she shares gem after gem of what helped her to come out of a debilitating depression and find love again after divorce.

The yellow sheets are filled with ink—and filled with hope. This is the first woman I've spoken to who success-fully recovered after a devastating heartbreak. These pages are a guide for me, not just in healing my broken heart, but starting to explore this newfound spiritual practice. Bud-dhism is so new to me, and she has given me the first steps to engage with it and actually use it in my life. I feel like I have actual steps I can take.

I just met this woman, and yet she has treated me as if she's known me for years.

I walk out and go home and immediately set up a small place in my apartment to chant, and put the yellow pages out for me to see every day.

I grab my journal and answer every question on the sheet, and some of the answers really surprise me.

How to Recover from Heartbreak
(Notes from Cathy)

1. Start with yourself and make yourself strong

2. Write out Six Sentences:

   I want _____

   I need _____

   I feel _____

   I am _____

   I'm afraid that _____

   I'm glad that _____

3. Have compassion with yourself. There is nothing unique about my situation, but my experience is unique, how I'm going about it. This doesn't change the pain.

4. Buddhism is being who you are.

5. Anger is a signpost. Ask these three questions of your anger. Say to your anger, tell me what you are here to tell me. Respect your anger by asking:

   ·Why am I angry?

   ·What am I angry about?

   ·What didn't I get?

6. Resentment is drinking poison and waiting for the other person to die.

7. Write a letter. Pour out everything I feel. Seal it with who I am, with care and nurturing. Then destroy it immediately. I have to admit everything I am feeling and then to know I am ok. I am worthy of love. Bring unconditional love and compassion to myself as I try to fill my life.

8. Feelings aren't facts.

9. I can't fix myself. I can only heal.

CONVERSATION

"BUDDHISM IS BEING WHO YOU ARE."

I look at this sentence on the sheet for what feels like the millionth time since being in Cathy's kitchen. And it's only been a few weeks. The chanting is helping.

"Buddhism is being who you are."

Ok… but who am I?

I feel like I am losing so much, and now I have NO idea who I am.

As I'm losing my marriage and am no longer a wife, then who am I?

As I'm no longer trying to get pregnant and become a mother, then who am I?

As I'm not auditioning and feel so disconnected as an artist, then who am I?

These questions burn like a hot fire within me, and I feel this deep thirst, like I have been in the desert for eternity. I open up my laptop and type in "teachings on Buddhism."

I click on a website packed with free audios from a female Tibetan teacher, and the first one goes right through me like a knife. My cursor is blinking on the lesson "Anger."

Anger. Oh… I know you. I feel like every day I am on a crazy see-saw of either bawling my eyes out in desperate heartbreak or wanting to set fire to everything around me. Sometimes it's overwhelming and so consuming. I've never felt this much anger in my life, and I don't know what to do with it.

Click.

As soon as she starts speaking, I grab my phone and start taking notes. My fingers are flying, every word is hitting home. I feel she is speaking directly to me, like we are hav-ing a conversation.

TEACHER:

Anger is the feeling. The behavior is the action.

Anger is the mental state where we exaggerate or proj-ect negative qualities on someone else until we can no longer endure. When I'm mad, I'm right!

Patience is the mind that is calm in the face of danger or abuse. It is the mental attitude. Not the behavior. Patience is not waiting, it is the inner feeling of calm. From that calm, we can decide our behavior. Aggres-sive behavior/passive behavior can be motivated by both anger and calm.

We want to actively be able to let go or transform anger, not suppress it.

ME:

Anger can be transformed? I want to learn this.

TEACHER:

If you're in the habit of releasing anger at a human being, it doesn't really deal with the anger, just the physical part of the anger.

ME:

Oh God, I did this. I did this all the time. I threw my anger at my ex. I thought I was just being honest.

TEACHER:

We say and do things under the influence of anger that are not helpful. We just say things the way they come out. Is this true communication? Is saying what we feel communication? We want to express something so the other person can understand it. When we are patient, we can do this. How do you feel about yourself after being angry? I got my revenge! Is that conducive for self respect? Do we feel good about ourselves when we hurt people intentionally?

ME:

I always felt worse. I keep thinking it's going to feel good, but it doesn't. I keep thinking I want to hurt my ex, but it always feels terrible. I just end up feeling so lost, and not getting what I want.

TEACHER:

You yell and scream at someone you love, then you destroy the trust. We believe our loved ones are so close to me that I can say whatever I want and they will always be there. This is not true. We forget and destroy our relationships.

ME:

I thought he would always be there… there is no trust anymore.

TEACHER:

Anger is not the only motivator to change things or intercede… compassion is. Don't confuse compassion with passivity or stupidity. Compassion is for self and others to be free of suffering. Compassion will bring a calmer mind and will bring solutions. When we inflict harm, the other person will only get angrier and keep doing whatever they are doing. Compassion can correct injustice by creating compassion for both sides.

We tend to think if we punish the people who hurt us they will stop because they will be nice to me through intimidation… this never works. It's going to trigger more attacks against us. Make an effort to listen with your heart to how the other person is perceiving the situation. How can we end conflict unless we understand the other's point of view?

We have to broaden our compassion. We need to see everyone equally wanting to be free of suffering and wanting happiness.

ME:

Everyone?? But he hurt me! He destroyed our marriage! He was a complete coward and wouldn't even work on it! He left me to do everything, just like he always did!

TEACHER:

Forgiving doesn't mean condoning. Forgiving means we are going to stop being angry at what was done. I'm going to let go of my anger because when I hold onto a grudge, I'm the one who hurts. I create the anger. We hold on to the resentment. Every time we remember it, we do it to ourselves again and again. We have our own court case. "I am right! How can I forgive if I'm right and the whole world is on my side?" You can be right, but you won't be happy. As long as I hold onto my resentment, it's self torture. Forgiving is the process of letting go of the anger in my heart. We can still say what they did was wrong, we just aren't angry.

"I hurt, I've been crying and they have to admit they were mean!" That mental state gives away my power. I have to let go of my wish for acknowledgement. What good does the acknowledgement actually do? Their apology doesn't do anything for me. Why should happiness be contingent on them? You will remember. But you don't have to hold a grudge to make your future better.

ME:

No apology? Then what do I have? How does the pain stop?

TEACHER:

See how someone is similar to yourself. Then the situation can move. We both want to be happy, we both want to be free of suffering.

I have to be satisfied with contributing what I can. I recognize I do not have control over what other people do.

ME:

I have no control over what my ex does. I thought I did. I truly thought I did. I think that's why it hurts so much. I was so wrong.

TEACHER:

The anger must be there before you deal with it. This is not repression.

ME:

Dealing with anger. Feeling my anger. This is new to me, especially as a woman. I was not taught how to do this. I was taught to throw my anger at someone else. Maybe that's part of the fire.

TEACHER:

There was a person who was shaking because no one had told him he could let go of his anger. Without that, he had no identity. Holding on to the anger is continuing abuse. You're trapped in being a victim.

The belief that letting go brings pain is the ego. Clinging brings the pain. Hurting others creates fear and just comes back as karma.

Stay connected. Don't doubt. Don't turn away.

ME:

(Weeping)

TEACHER:

Stay connected. Don't doubt. Don't turn away.

ME:

(Weeping)

TEACHER:

"There is nothing outside to blame." — The Buddha

Spiritual path requires absolute honesty. Letting go comes from wisdom of what you're holding on to.

"What is happening to me right now is perfect and exactly what I need to learn. Problems show me what I have to do. I can deal with it." Whatever comes, let it come. Whatever goes, let it go.

Resistance = suffering.

Acceptance that comes from wisdom = courage

You are perfect within yourself. Clinging to things we think are precious and we think we need = suffering.

What am I losing if I let go?

ME:

Stay connected, don't turn away.

Stay connected, don't turn away.

Stay connected, don't turn away.

Who am I if I let go?

Who am I?

"SO, THE FIRST STEP is to divide the bank accounts."

I literally feel as if my whole body is tearing apart. I ask to go to the bathroom, and as soon as I'm inside, I stuff tissues in my mouth to keep from screaming.

This was all my idea.

I spoke with a divorce lawyer, and when she heard the situation, she recommended mediation. "This is pretty straightforward, and if he's willing, it will be the least expensive and also most humane way of ending things."

No courts.

No allegations.

Just the two of us working with a mediation team, sitting across from each other and negotiating how to move forward.

I sounded so calm when I spoke to the mediation lawyers, set up the appointment, and convinced my husband.

And yet, this was probably the worst experience of my life.

I felt like I was sitting across from a stranger. And not a tear from his eyes. Just me, excusing myself again and again to have another breakdown in the bathroom as we went through the process.

Here I was, again taking control in the marriage, and how ironic, in our divorce. Even though he didn't want to save the marriage, apparently he didn't want to put any energy into ending it either. It was excruciating.

I was the driver in my own heartbreak.

Sitting back down with a pile of tissues in front of me, the two lawyers look at me with compassionate eyes and ask if it is all right to continue.

My husband is not even making eye contact with me. He's just holding his pen and staring at the yellow legal pad in front of him.

"Yes," I meekly whisper.

I'm taking notes on what I need to do next, but my sight keeps blurring and the paper is getting soaked.

"Ok, we will reconvene in two weeks."

My husband and I haven't been living together for weeks. I've been staying at our apartment, and he is staying at a mutual friend's.

My mother flew out very quickly in January and just held me over the weekend. We were both trying to make sense of what was happening.

We were both still in love with him.

Now, in February, she was returning to help me divide everything up, to make an inventory that I could take to the next mediation and create an agreement.

An agreement that I literally didn't want. I didn't want any of this. I didn't want to sell our apartment. I didn't want to divide up our things. I didn't want to end our marriage.

I was not in agreement, and yet I was the driving force in creating it.

When I began to totally unload all of my pain in therapy, my therapist took one look at me and said, "Wow. You must be exhausted." And it was as if I had never realized how much I was the go-getter in the marriage. How much I was the cheerleader, and most of all, how no matter the depth or enthusiasm I would express in his ability and talents, he never believed in himself.

One partner with a growth mindset, and one partner who is passive aggressive. Not a great match. Probably the only way we stayed married so long was because we spent so much time apart. Apparently, the fact that I grew up in a military home and moved every 1-3 years put me in the perfect position to create a long-distance relationship. I had become so used to adapting to my environment that I had no idea what true stability felt like.

Jon and I had made the decision that we would never be apart from each other for more than 3–5 weeks, but last year with both of us working non-stop at different theaters, we broke our rule over and over. Our marriage consisted of more time apart than together.

My therapist said, "If you'd had day-to-day life together, this would have happened much sooner."

Oh... I think she's right.

Now, I actually had an incredible amount of resentment and anger coming to the surface that had been lurking underneath. I found my days to be a constant see-saw of seething anger towards him for destroying everything and complete panic that I couldn't stop the momentum of everything going up in smoke.

My safety and security were gone. I felt terrified. I wanted to have a family and had just spent 19 years with a man who I thought wanted to have one too. So, here I stood in my late 30s looking at having to start all over again.

Oh God... why didn't I leave sooner?

Why did I hang on so tight?

When the doorbell rings, my mother, fresh from the airport, takes one look at me, and we silently weep in a deep embrace.

"Ok," she says, rolling up her sleeves. "Let's go to work."

And then I watch my mother start to take everything out of the kitchen cabinets. Every dish that she had actually organized and set up when we moved in here 8 years ago and became homeowners for the first time.

The whole family had come to make it happen: parents, aunts and uncles and cousins. My mother-in-law made her famous chicken corn soup, my mother made her delicious chocolate chip cookies, and everyone gathered to celebrate us actually buying a co-op. Renters to homeowners, a building with a washing machine, an actual elevator, and a very small second bedroom that would be our office, but we knew could easily convert it to a baby's room. While loading all our boxes from Astoria to Jackson Heights, we laughed and shared in the communal cheering to a bright future.

We shared as a family.

Seeing the ghosts of that homecoming party still standing in the kitchen, my mother takes dish after dish out that she actually bought us; dishes she helped scoop food onto as she laughed with my husband by the countertops, sharing her favorite techniques. Cook to cook, mother to son.

I'm not just losing him. I'm losing a family.

We both are.

I grab a legal pad and follow her, right into the middle of the ghosts.

EYE SHADOW

"YOU ARE ALL SET!"

The teller smiles at me, and I realize my stomach has been tied in knots the whole last hour I was setting up my own bank account.

I haven't had my own account since I was 22, right before I got married.

Now, the only name I see is mine.

There's not much in the account, but I actually feel lighter.

Years of stressing over every purchase and getting approval are melting away.

I push the doors open and walk out onto 23rd Street in midtown Manhattan.

Right across is a CVS, and I remember I need soap, so I cross the street.

Soap in hand, I pass the makeup aisle and look down at a sparkling green eyeshadow. And in that moment, I decide to buy it.

Something for me.

No permission needed.

My first purchase as a single woman.

This actually feels good.

I am completely surprised.

13

Birdwings

Your grief for what you've lost lifts a mirror
up to where you're bravely working.

Expecting the worst, you look and instead,
here's the joyful face you've been wanting to see.

Your hand opens and closes and opens and closes.

If it were always a fist or always stretched open,
you would be paralyzed.

Your deepest presence is in every small contracting
and expanding,

the two as beautifully balanced and coordinated
as birdwings.

— Rumi

BATHROOM

IT'S HAPPENING AGAIN. I feel a wave of shock come over my whole body as the simple sentence blazes across my brain, "You are getting a divorce."

Hot tears start to crest at my eyes, and I'm fighting them back. I'm in a cubicle at work right now, but at any moment my temp contact could come around the corner to check on me or ask for something while I'm working on this project.

I have to pull it together.

No one here really knows me. I'm just here for a week or two. No one knows my whole life is falling apart. No one knows how horrible it is to be in my apartment alone, the ghost of my marriage in every corner. I can't seem to escape, and just staring at any piece of furniture in our home brings up a hundred sweet memories I desperately don't want to let go of.

As I feel the heat rising through my whole body and start to shake, I quickly dart for the bathroom. I close the stall and sit down, and place my hand on my heart.

It literally hurts, like a stabbing knife right in the middle of my chest. It's been like this since Thanksgiving, and my constant cough doesn't help. It feels like there is a knot, twisted so tight and gnarled. This is what my heart has become.

I've been devouring everything I can on Buddhism, and in this moment of panic and complete embarrassment, I try something new instead of fighting.

I say YES.

I say YES to the pain in my heart.

I say YES to the fact that I am getting a divorce.

I say YES to locking myself in the bathroom stall during a temp office job to gather myself.

I say YES to where I am and what I am feeling.

And a miracle happens.

The knot loosens. My sobs quiet, and for a minute, my heart actually stops hurting. I feel my chest open and some space come in.

I can't believe that worked...

I return to the bathroom again later that day, and the next, and the next.

March 8, 2013 1:11 pm
Sender: Mom
Subject line: home

Hi again,

Your home is not a healthy or happy place to be - and lacks the love that made it so very special.

Every time we moved in the military, although we hated leaving our "homes"—they were actually no more than houses—places to live—"home" is where the heart is... and right now your heart needs sanctuary and a safe place apart from what is called home. Now it is time to move to a new place—make a new home, new experiences and look towards a brighter day and future. Saw a one-minute video on the last survivor from the Holocaust who is 109— her approach to life is optimism—to look for beauty—be aware of the bad things and ugly things around you, but there is beauty everywhere to see and behold and taking joy and happiness from that beauty is what has helped her throughout her life.

I wish that all the beauty that surrounds you envelops you and brings you peace.

Love, Mom

Out beyond ideas of wrongdoing and rightdoing,
there is a field. I'll meet you there.

When the soul lies down in that grass,
the world is too full to talk about.

Ideas, language, even the phrase each other
doesn't make sense.

— Rumi

POEM

MY BAGS ARE ALL PACKED. Surveying the apartment, I take in the space that has been my home for the last 8 years.

After a very aggressive and horrible second mediation where I saw the absolute worst of my husband, the third and final meeting seemed to bring an actual agreement.

This list is his.

This list is mine.

I'll go live at a friend's for three months while he lives here and packs up his things before the closing on June 1st.

Our apartment sold within a week. The process was all underway that quickly.

And it's only the beginning of March. This storm is raging fast, very fast, moving at a pace that leaves me every day in continual shock.

I'm getting a divorce.

I'm getting a divorce.

And I don't know if I'll ever stop coughing.

And looking at my bags, I know there is one final piece before I leave.

I grab a writing pad, and five simple words emerge from my pen: "take a trip with me." I am immediately transported back to the only other time I wrote them, in an empty bathroom when I was 18 years old on closing night.

This was my first professional show, the summer after my freshman year at college, and I was devastated it was over. Mostly because it meant I had to say goodbye, and this was the only way I knew how.

I had watched Jon for the whole school year, enraptured at his performances, and swept up in his handsome face and long muscular body. My whole being came alive whenever I saw him in the theater department halls, and when we were cast together in the summer musical, I was so excited.

I was also in a serious long-distance relationship with my boyfriend at University of Virginia.

But the first week of rehearsal, our eyes found each other. And soon, we were finding every excuse to spend lunch breaks together.

And then nights.

I fell madly in love with Jon, and just before closing, he admitted he felt the same. But I had a boyfriend, and he was heading to Chicago to do a show and then moving to New York. This was just now. Love or not.

So, I wrote a poem to him, beginning with this stanza:

> *Take a trip with me*
> *through my mind*
> *and over time*
>
> *Close your eyes*
> *and stare forever at a glimpse*
> *of happiness*
> *of truth*
> *of core emotions*
>
> *Strip the wall*
> *unlock the door*
> *"I'm here for you"......*

We cried in each other's arms that last night into the early hours of the morning, and he loved every word I wrote.

And then I returned home, and as soon as I saw my boy-friend, I knew I had to tell him. We broke up a week later, and I called up Jon, who was in Chicago doing a show, and asked him with a confident fervor, "What do you want?"

I drove the train. In that instant, I created our four-year long-distance relationship, our engagement, and wedding that occurred two weeks after I graduated college.

I was convinced he was my soulmate. I was convinced he was going to be the father of my children, and we would hold hands until our dying days.

I had my maid of honor sing the theme from the classic movie *An Affair to Remember* at our wedding. This was all kismet.

And now, with signed mediation papers, and the state of New York legalizing our divorce, I was experiencing a very different effect of an affair.

His affair.

My affair.

We began our relationship with an affair and ended it with the same. Both of us.

"Affairs are acts of anger," my therapist said.

How long had I been angry?

How long had he?

I'm recognizing how exhausting controlling my husband is, and I wouldn't wish this on anyone.

I look down at the poem, now written at the kitchen table in the home I am leaving. It reads like a history of our coming together, our most beautiful moments, and this gaping divide that has ripped us apart.

Folding it into an envelope, I leave it for him.

Just like I did when I was 18, when I thought I was saying goodbye and wanted to memorialize our special time together. Now the story holds the full picture.

But this time, there won't be a phone call a week later to ask him what he wants. I asked that in Salt Lake, and his answer was very clear. I'm not going to ask anymore.

This time, I know it really is the end.

Untitled

Take a trip with me
 from a fountain
  to a park
 baskets in celebration
  and surprises with balloons

Fly over market places
 where berbers roam smiling

Glide through our legs
 as we dance
 cheek to cheek
 on a simple carpet of white

There, in a tree
 a hawk turns its head
 surveying before beating its wings
 and taking to the air,
  witnessed and recognized.

There, on a chair
 sit two lovers as they survey
 a perfect Maine sunset

There, on a step, eyes wide in wonder
 as lights twinkle forming a
 giant champagne tower of lights
  hourly

We clasped hands as children
 growing into adults
 forging our hearts
  our futures
 as we sipped Oxford tea

We dreamed
   we stepped
      we linked
         we planned

Crystal hung from the window
Silk draped our furniture and walls
   Music poured from our mouths
   professing undying love

Then the tiles cracked
   and fear stepped into our home
   covering our hearts
   and planting seeds of doubt

Minds contracted and spun
   spiraling without guidance
      layering upon themselves
         and embedding secrets
         and silence

The hawk clung on to the branch
The tea turned bitter
   scalding our lips,
And lightbulbs slowly burned out
   one by one

Suddenly a cliff
a leap required and duality became single
   the boat once expansive became
      so small
         constricted under the pressure
         of time and regret
      strangling the magic
         the hopes
            and the desires

Hands separated and a divide
   grew, one choosing to step backwards
   one, clutching and begging

      Imbalance
      Imperfect
      loss
      grief, denial, passivity
      and breaking

   The trip, at an end
   no longer inhabited by two

Above the stars
looked down
upon their souls
   and wept
in remembrance
   a steady slow rain

While the moon
   shone radiance
      in care
      in sweet compassion
   bathing them each
      in a ray of love,
   whispering simply
      "fear no more"

STEP 2
DHAMMA VICAYA

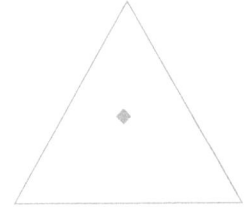

Observation of Experience

SILENCE

THE DOOR CLOSES BEHIND ME, and I hear my friends' footsteps head down the hallway towards the elevator.

My bags lay all in front of me, most of my possessions, or at least what I will need for the next three months. All lovingly brought up with the help of my friend and her husband who picked me up early this morning in Jackson Heights and drove me to Inwood, to our mutual friends' apartment, which will be my new home for now.

I turn my head and look into the kitchen and remember the conversation we had two months ago in January.

"It's all over. I'm getting a divorce and we have to sell our apartment. Neither of us can afford to pay for it by ourselves, and honestly, I don't want to be there. It's torture."

And with warm, big eyes, Beth looked at me and said, "You can live here. We won't be here for three months because Ted is going to school, and we will be living with my in-laws in Vermont. Stay here while you find your own place."

I had never loved Beth more than in that moment. I had come up here to tell her what was going on. I never thought to ask if I could stay in her apartment and was floored at this generous offer.

My life was falling apart, but I was experiencing so much generosity from my loved ones. I actually had the keys to five different apartments on my key ring. So many friends stepped forward when they heard.

Turning my head back towards the living room, I slowly walk in to take in what will be my new home for the spring. I had always loved Beth's apartment. Two bedrooms and so alive with the joy of her two young children whose smiling faces and colorful artwork adorn the bookshelves and fridge.

And all I hear is silence.

Sweet silence.

Oh... I'm finally out of there. Thank God.

And I let out the largest exhale. I think I've been holding my breath for months.

Curfews

Noise
Is a cruel ruler

Who is always imposing
Curfews,

While Stillness and quiet
Break open the vintage
Bottles,

Awake the real
Band.

— Hafiz

NIKÓL ROGERS

TV

SITTING ON THE COUCH, I stare at Beth's huge flatscreen TV. Poised in the air, my hand holds the remote as I remember the small rectangle I stared at for years in my home.

I always loved TV. I loved all the stories, the characters, the adventures, and most of all, sharing them with my husband.

So many nights, he would lay across the couch, and I would take the easy chair, and we would devour weekly network tales. And I loved talking about it afterwards; something we could share, a passion that brought us closer.

But over the years, I found myself watching more and more shows by myself. He would be working in the office and only intermittently come out. Our DVR filled up, and I would feel anxious at the back-up. I had so many shows going, how was I going to be able to watch them all?

Why didn't he want to watch them with me anymore?

Our nights were turning into dinner and then TV and bed.

So, in response, I just watched more TV. What else was there to do? I couldn't tell him about my affair, or yell at him one more time about how I felt like he was scared to have children or how unhappy I was in my career.

The stories and characters helped me forget for an hour or three what was going on.

Beth's TV looms in front of me, a reminder of how I distracted myself from what was really happening: my marriage falling apart.

I put down the remote and decide to take a break from TV.

The silence surrounding me feels like a loving embrace, and I feel my body sink into the couch with relief.

ONE WEEK

I'VE BEEN LIVING AT BETH'S for one week, and my cough is gone.

Completely.

I guess I do have very strong lungs.

I just needed a new environment, and to breathe in something very different.

This air is actually opening my throat, not closing it.

Quietness

Inside this new love, die.

Your way begins on the other side.

Become the sky.

Take an axe to the prison wall.

Escape.

Walk out like someone suddenly born into color.

Do it now.

You're covered with thick cloud.

Slide out the side. Die,
and be quiet. Quietness is the surest sign
that you've died.

Your old life was a frantic running
from silence.

The speechless full moon
comes out now.

— Rumi

WISDOM

SITTING IN BETH'S APARTMENT after a long day of temping in an office, I reach for my computer. I've been reading the female Tibetan teacher's words about anger over and over and feeling such a call for silence.

Something is opening in me, and I stare at Rumi's poem, his words like a knife through me, *"Your old life was a frantic running from silence."*

Yet now, it's all I desire.

I am also so hungry for guidance and have been reading as many books as I can on Buddhism. What is this change beginning in me?

I open the portal online for the Tibetan teacher, and one word pops forward, so I click on that lesson and grab my phone to take notes again. I feel her here with me in the dark and quiet of the living room. Our conversation begins.

TEACHER:

Emptiness.

Wisdom is emptiness.

The nature of the mind is empty, not threatening, cold, or vacuous.

If you take apart a watch, where is the watch? The watch is several dependent pieces put together and then labeled by us.

You can never find the thing in itself, just the designations we have decided upon.

ME:

(listening)

TEACHER:

Each of us is made up of a body, mind, thoughts, judgments, likes, opinions… and to each of those, we say "me." My head, my ideas, my hopes, my fears. But if we look for the "I" behind all the "me-ness," where do you find it?

ME:

I have no idea… I never considered that.

TEACHER:

Meditation is about stripping the layers of the onion. We have so much false identification. We ignore the genuine reality. Outwardly we appear prosperous, but inside are lacking, lacking genuine self confidence. What are people escaping from?

ME:

What am I escaping from?

TEACHER:

We meditate to be able to see into the nature of the mind. Wisdom doesn't mean knowing about, wisdom is becoming what we have actually experienced and realized.

ME:

This is what wisdom is?

TEACHER:

Our body is changing moment to moment, cells constantly recycling. If we lose a hair, we are not the hair. We are not the body. Thoughts arise and then are gone. Rising, falling. What do we identify with? Which bit is the "me"? Wisdom is dealing with "who am I?" The whole world revolves around "I." We are engrossed in our own movie. What if we turned around and instead of looking at the screen, we would see little transparent frames of film and light? If we look out, we see what is projected out.

Meditation is to turn our focus inwards. What we see is a stream of thoughts, like the frames and lights. As the awareness grows, the waterfall slows down and becomes a slow river. If we continue to watch our thoughts, they become more transparent. If our awareness is clear and the mind is relaxed, we will see a gap... an inner light shining through, and a direct awareness of our primordial nature. Once this is seen, we see how confused we are and confused and desperate others are. We are so confused about our identity. Compassion arises because we see the problem and how we cling with our mind and create suffering.

ME:

A gap...

TEACHER:

Meditation brings us back to where we have never left.

ME:

A place I never left... this has been here all along?

TEACHER:

Liberation lies in reconnecting with our true being again. Learning how to be present.

We have to encourage the goodness to grow, our kindness and understanding have to be watered. Each one of us has a wisdom mind, but we have to uncover it with greater mental clarity and an open heart, free of fear.

ME:

(frantically writing) I have to uncover it.

TEACHER:

When dealing with a conflict or enemy: look at your motivation behind your actions. If it is rooted in anger or frustration, us against them, then you are only perpetuating the cycle. If the motivation is genuine compassion, then it's good. If you stay too passive, then very negative forces take over.

ME:

(silence)

(silence)

(silence)

Dream Journal
3/24/13

I dreamt I was walking with Jon, and it was a familiar situation of
trying to convince him of my point of view and him not agreeing or
wanting to work on us. I yell at him just as he is on a small ledge,
while pulling a curtain open with my hand, which causes him to fall.
He crumples into a broken mess, and his neck is broken, but he's
still alive. I panic and tell him to stay where he is, I'll get help. I start
running around calling for help and see him up and walking away as if
nothing happened.

DANTE

I WALK INTO A BIG ROOM, sunlight flooding in through the windows, as the sounds of a Manhattan Sunday echo through the panes.

Before me is a circle of dark navy meditation cushions, mostly filled with people having conversations. I spy an empty one and sit down.

My search for Buddhism was continuing in full force after devouring several books and listening to the Buddhist teacher online. I had come to a Tibetan Buddhist Center for beginning instruction on meditation a week ago and loved the space. When I looked at their website, something caught my eye.

A healing support group.

Led by a Buddhist teacher named Jason, the group centered around the concept that, no matter what, healing was possible.

As my heart continued to ache in my chest every day, this struck me. Therapy was making a huge difference for me, and I wondered if a group could also help me recover.

Except I was terrified.

I'd never been to a support group before.

Sitting on the cushion in between two people who were very involved in a conversation about drug trips from the 70s, I feel myself panic. I only smoked some pot for fun in college, I never did hard drugs. Am I in the right place?

I'm about to bolt from the room when right at that moment, a fluffy Pomeranian bounds towards me. A ball of rusty joy, the dog snuggles up to me. I love animals and immediately start petting his long, soft fur.

"That's Dante," I hear. I look up and see a woman across the circle from me in a motorized wheelchair, smiling at me.

"He's adorable," I offer meekly. I look at Dante and silently say, "Ok, I guess I will stay." In response, he splays out in front of me so I can rub his belly.

"All right, everyone, let's settle in and get started. We will begin with 20 minutes of meditation. If you haven't received beginning instruction, I'll walk you through it." Jason hits the gong.

Dante saunters to the middle of the circle, plopping down with ease, splaying out his legs and settling his stomach on the shining wood floor. I close my eyes.

Focus on breathing in.

Focus on breathing out.

WHAT AM I DOING HERE?

Focus on breathing in.

Focus on breathing out.

I DON'T KNOW ANYONE HERE.

Focus on breathing in.

Focus on breathing out.

I AM SO SCARED.

And then I feel a wet sensation on my left ring finger and realize Dante has set himself at my left knee. He gently licks my bare finger again and again, and I start to weep. The phantom of my wedding ring now before me, a scene starts to play, beginning with when I first saw the sparkling band.

In my memory, I hear Jon say, "Ok, you can open your eyes."

———————————

I'm sitting on a stage, and Jon is holding my hand after leading me here blindfolded. As I look around, I see the set for the most recent play happening on the main stage at Penn State, and things start to come into focus.

"I wanted to ask you to marry me in the same place I first said I love you." His eyes are so big, and I start to cry. I can't see, everything is blurry, and I realize he's kneeling. He pulls out a box and holds the most beautiful ring up to me, asking the words I have been waiting to hear for four years: "Will you marry me?"

And I'm speechless. He did it. He bought me a beautiful ring. He had me convinced we were using the ring from my great grandmother. Yes, her ring was small, but he was an aspiring actor in NYC and working at a restaurant. I never thought he could afford it.

And yet, here it was.

I choke out a yes, and we kiss and kiss. The happiest moment of my life! Oh YES! I want to marry you, Jon! I want to spend the rest of my life with you!

———————————

At first, wearing the ring my senior year of college was like a dream come true, but I found myself attracted to other men, men I was in shows with. In the spring, just months before our wedding, I kissed my leading man in the spring musical and was horrified. What was I doing? Didn't I want to be married to Jon?

As soon as it happened, I told Jon about it, and he asked if we should postpone the wedding. I begged him not to and took all of my doubts and shoved them so deep.

So deep.

Except they came out raging in our first year of marriage. Raging like fire storms out of my mouth, with escalating fights. My parents came to visit, and my mother pulled me aside after watching an interaction between us with deep concern.

"Mom, this is what a healthy relationship looks like," I snapped. "You and dad never fight. He just yells at you, and you stay silent. I'm speaking my mind. This is what equality looks like."

The fights did lessen as the distance increased. Over the years, with both of us working consistently in regional theaters, we made that agreement to never go longer than three and a half weeks without seeing each other. And oh, how sweet the reunions were, fiery and exciting. But long-term day-to-day was not the norm.

And I continued to find myself attracted to other men when I was in shows. I had no idea why. But I felt pride that nothing happened. I was in control.

Wasn't I?

I wasn't cheating, until I met Dan. I had just celebrated my 10-year wedding anniversary. A huge milestone, and we took the trip of a lifetime to Paris. Three years of my child-hood were spent in Belgium since my father was stationed at an international military base, and we took regular trips to Paris. It was my favorite international city. Sharing it with Jon was sheer joy. We ate baguettes, kissed in Montmartre, and sat at streetside cafes sipping tea. It was so romantic.

But when we returned home, Jon went to a theater for the summer in Missouri, and when he came home, he wouldn't stop talking about his co-star, Cassie. I had never heard him talk about another woman before, and suddenly, they were texting all the time, and my whole being knew something was off. I confronted him, and he told me noth-ing happened. I didn't believe him, so when I went off to do a Christmas show in 2008, I showed up to the first day of rehearsal and looked around the room, scanning for the handsome men.

And there was Dan.

There was Dan.

After a drunken night, I was shocked. I couldn't believe what I had done. I didn't understand, so I just drank again, and even more. I told no one. The only person who knew was Dan, and when we both got back to the city I met him for drinks and looked him in the eyes, pleading with him, "Why did I do this?"

His response, "Things happen."

And then things happened off and on for four years. All while wearing my ring and convincing myself I could control this. I had to hide this. I could lose everything.

And then, Jon kneeled in front of me on this last Thanksgiving Day and told me he was in love with another co-star, from the same theater he had worked at in 2008. It wasn't Cassie, but she looked exactly like her. Shannon and Cassie could have been sisters.

And the next day, I took off my ring.

Now, Dante was licking my ring finger, the place that was hurting the most. The place that was so twisted in shame, confusion and anger.

Tears falling, falling, falling, the stage disappearing from view as Jason rings the gong and brings us all back from meditation.

"Ok, everyone. We have some new faces, so we will pass the mic around. If you feel comfortable, please share your name and what brought you to the group today."

My insides are tying into knots as I watch the mic pass from person to person.

And I look at my finger and at Dante and make a decision to do something I've never done publicly before.

When the mic comes to me, I decide to tell the truth.

Words are spilling out of me, and I'm crying, vulnerably sharing why I am here and what is happening right now in my life.

And after I finish, I witness a miracle.

I see and feel people coming closer to me. And I watch each person after me then share more openly where they are and what they are struggling with. And I feel that same opening inside my body I felt in the bathroom during my temp job.

And I realize I've been wrong. All these years of my life, on stage and in my relationships, I had always thought if I was vulnerable and honest, I would be rejected. I thought people would leave me and hate me, and yet here I was seeing the exact opposite. It wasn't the hiding that brought people closer, it was vulnerability.

Oh, I've been hiding for so long. I've been acting for so long, because I thought no one would accept me as I was.

After the meeting is over, I go up to Jason to sign up for his mailing list because I want to come back every month. And he looks up at me with these big blue eyes and says, "That was very courageous."

Oh... is this what courage is?

I hug him with all my heart and say, "Thank you for your teaching. I'll be back next month."

I watch Dante gleefully exit the room with his owner and then grab my backpack and walk out into the March sun.

CLOSET

LOOKING AT MY CLOTHES hanging in Beth's closet, I see brown, brown, and more brown. Some variations of dark colors, some creams and ivories, but everything is dark.

How long has my wardrobe been like this?

I've lost a lot of weight, and my attempts at gaining it with ice cream don't seem to be working.

My sleep is still really erratic, and most nights I'm waking up in full body sweats from disturbing dreams.

I am eating again, but my body is the thinnest it's been since I was a teen.

I decide to go buy some comfortable clothing, something new that actually feels good on my skin. Something soft, not something Jon bought me.

I find myself in the organic section of a discount store and see bright turquoise. When I touch the soft cotton sleeve, I feel my body calm.

I don't think I've had turquoise in my wardrobe since I was a teenager.

I think it's time for some color.

Swimming
3/20/13

A lake,
a battle
and yet I am alone on the side,
simply witnessing
anger, rage, and pure human destruction
of women and men.

I turn and begin to swim
within calm waters,
within my own lane,
removed from the warring churn.

At my side,
a form swims
beneath the surface
never sipping for breath
but continuously moving in the water
peacefully
simultaneously
as I swim forward.

SUBWAY

IT'S A LONG SUBWAY ride from Inwood to midtown. I hop on the 1 train at 242nd Street and settle in with the other morning commuters, quickly grabbing a seat and avoiding any eye contact.

Thankfully, I have friends for the next hour: Rumi and Hafiz. I bought these poetry collections from my yoga studio and keep dog-earing the pages. Almost every poem is speaking to me.

As they have for years.

My favorite period of the day in third grade was creative writing. I couldn't wait to grab the lined paper and bring the pencil to the page in front of me. Stories flowed so easily, and I was encouraged by my teacher and mother who both handed my stories back to me with tears in their eyes.

And then I found poetry in eleventh grade, or poetry bellowed to me.

"This is the poet's circle!" my English teacher exclaimed loudly. Over six feet tall, and also the basketball coach, he stood in the center of the classroom after having us rearrange our desks to create a giant square. Taking out a large piece of white chalk, he drew a circle around himself and looked at us with fire in his eyes, challenging us, "Are you in or out?"

My whole being shouted, and I rose from my chair declaring, "I am IN! I am in the poet's circle!"

I was filling journals with poems, and when I fell in love with Jon, it was as if a floodgate opened. I wrote them all the time. In my 20s, I met a mentor who introduced me to the Pennsylvania Poetry Society, and I even had a poem published in their monthly publication.

But mostly, I kept my poetry very private. I didn't think I had what it took to really be a writer professionally, and I believed my father when he said I would never make any money from my writing, so my poetry stayed just for loved ones. I wrote poems for my husband, my close friends, and a Christmas poem for my family every year. It was a joy, but I never went further.

Now, holding the books as close to me as possible, I run my finger over the page as I cry, closing my eyes and hunching over. So much beauty in these words, speaking directly to my aching heart so in need of healing and love.

I look up from the page for a moment and see a man sitting across from me with his head in his hands, sunk over in pain. I take him in and think, "Wow, he looks exactly how I feel."

For months, I had been riding the subway trying to hide my tears, trying to hold it together, seeing people holding hands and laughing and just feeling so alone. And here in one instant was a man who was struggling, just like me.

Much like the support group, I again feel this space between us. I feel what we are sharing in this moment, and realize I have so much more in common with people than differences.

I'm not alone.

Oh, sweet relief.

I watch the man leave the subway car, and I look around, taking in everyone truly for the first time that morning.

We are the mirror as well as the face in it.
We are tasting the taste this minute
of eternity. We are pain
and what cures pain, both. We are
the sweet cold water and the jar that pours.

This moment this love comes to rest in me,
many beings in one being.
In one wheat grain a thousand sheaf stacks.
Inside the needle's eye a turning night of stars.

Something opens our wings. Something
makes boredom and hurt disappear.
Someone fills the cup in front of us.
We taste only sacredness.

— Rumi

INTRO

I'M SITTING AT A SINGLE reception desk, facing a door to the hallway that leads to the elevators. Dark paint on the walls, fake plants, and a few chairs for visiting guests, I am alone in this entryway to the publishing house where I work as a temp.

The doors in front and behind me require guests to be buzzed in, or accessed through an employee pass. The room feels small, and actually feels comforting to me.

The phone is barely ringing, and I'm grateful for an easy day and for the work.

March is coming to a close, and I can feel a deep fatigue in my body and heart. Mediation is over, I'm all settled at Beth's, and the long subway commute is feeling more familiar.

But, I really want a getaway. The divorce is everywhere. And while my cough is gone now, I'm waking up most nights drenched from sweating, and my chest hurts most days.

I start to search online for weekend retreats, but the prices are way above what I can do right now.

And then I remember sitting in Cathy's after she taught me to chant, and her mentioning a place she went to when she was recovering from a debilitating depression. I pull out my Rumi collection of poetry from my backpack and find the three bright yellow sheets of paper I wrote all her notes on as we had tea.

And there at the bottom I see where I wrote it, a Zen monastery north of the city.

I look online and see they have an intro to Zen Training weekend, and there is one spot left.

I take it without hesitation and immediately feel some relief.

It's a week away.

Thank goodness. I could use some Zen in my life right now.

TISSUES

SITTING IN THE DARK surrounded by other people, I am feeling nervous. We've been sitting Zazen, the Zen form of meditation, and it's been so wonderful, but I know I'm going to be called soon to speak to the Abbott, to ask him my question in face-to-face teaching.

In Zen, it's called Dokusan, and the monastics have taught us how to enter the room, and invited us to bring a burning question to the teacher.

The question is so alive in my throat, I feel like I am choking on it, and I am terrified of what will happen when it actually comes out of my mouth.

I hear the monitor call my row, and I grab my cushion and get in line.

My heart is literally racing in my chest.

I hear the bell ring, the teacher signaling from behind the closed door that it is my time to enter, and I stumble up and come into the Abbott's room.

As he sits on a cushion calmly in the center of the room, I bow in concert with the retreat participant who was there before me, feel them then leave the room, and I do one more bow and then sit across from the Zen teacher.

He is staring right through me, and I know this is my moment to ask the question that has been burning a hole in my chest.

Opening my mouth, it spills out, "How do you let go?"

The pain of my divorce, my husband refusing to speak to me—completely shutting me out of his life after 18 years together—all erupts, and I can't stop crying. The flood has broken, and tears run down my face, creating a wet current of all my pain.

The Zen teacher looks at me and grabs a box of tissues and lays them in front of me. Then he looks me right in the eye and asks, "Are you ok without him?"

And everything stops. The tears stop. The flood stops and I blink. Because I realize in that moment that I am ok. I'm breathing. I'm alive. It's as if I've just woken from a bad dream.

I had thought I would physically die without him. I had even considered harming myself because I didn't think I could handle getting a divorce. Huddled in my old apartment back in December, I considered jumping out the window. And yet, here I was. The divorce didn't kill me.

I was alive.

I am alive.

I make my way back to my seat and feel an opening in my body.

And I am completely clear on two things.

One, I have found my practice; this is what I was seeking. Everything about Zen feels right to me. I had spent the last three months trying all different kinds of meditation and Buddhist practices, but this was the first time it felt like a full YES in my body.

And two, I know I want to live.

I want to live. And I want my life to look very different than it did.

The bell rings to signal the end of the meditation period and the end of our day, and a lone female monastic's voice sings out the Evening Gatha:

Let me respectfully remind you,

Life and death are of supreme importance.

Time swiftly passes by and opportunity is lost.

Each of us should strive to awaken...

Awaken... take heed!

Do not squander your life!

Tears are falling now, but they are no longer tears of pain.

I rise from my cushion and make my way to my dorm, climbing up into my bed, and close my eyes, falling asleep deeply for the first time in months.

The way of love is not
a subtle argument.

The door there
is devastation.

Birds make great sky-circles
of their freedom.
How do they learn it?

They fall, and falling,
they're given wings.

— Rumi

LUNCH

HOLDING MY PLATE AND CUP, I survey the dining hall of the monastery and choose to sit over at a new table among my fellow retreat participants.

I feel so refreshed after last night's sleep and so excited to dive into Zen fully. I want to learn everything!

A tall monastic sits next to me and turns gently and asks me where I came from and what I do. After fully sharing about my performing career and how wonderful the week-end is, I return the question.

"I split my time between here and the temple," he replies.

"The temple?" I ask.

"Yes, we have a sister temple in Brooklyn."

Oh my gosh, it's Christmas. I had no idea how I was going to regularly drive over two hours north of the city for retreats and service at the monastery. Now I can ride the subway instead.

Queens to Brooklyn.

I clear my plate and go buy a meditation bench from the Monastery store, already imagining the altar I'm going to create.

STEP 3
VIRIYA

Strength

THURSDAY

IT WAS SUPPOSED TO HAPPEN on Friday, or Saturday. Just not on Thursday.

Not on the 30th.

But our lawyer was going out of town and had to change the date she was meeting up with Jon. I had already signed the separation agreement, and it needed to be completed with his signature before closing.

But, at the last minute, she called Jon and asked to meet him because she was going out of town. Could he sign the papers today, Thursday?

May 30th.

So, he did, because there was no other choice.

On our 15-year wedding anniversary, he signed the papers to legally separate us and begin divorce within the state of New York.

The same day we walked down the aisle in blissful love.

Our marriage began and ended on the exact same day.

Was this planned?

Notes from therapy on Letting Go

Acknowledge the anger.

Investigate what I feel enchanted by as there might be an aspect of gratification or disappearing from the situation.

I need to weigh whether it is more painful to keep something or to become interested in the exit and way out.

I have to admit what I get out of anger before I can let it go. If I haven't learned to feel energy from another source than anger, I won't stop using anger. I need to admit the kick I get out of the "thing" before letting go.

Look at the hidden advantages of anger and don't pretend it's not hurting me and others. Look at the experience of suffering, caused by yourself and others. Find other ways to feel power than from anger. Bear with the pain and investigate in the moment of feeling anger.

In the face of anxiety, be present.

What can I feel?

What do I know?

ORNAMENT

I HAVE NEVER FELT MORE GRATEFUL for the family and friends in my life.

My brother showed up yesterday, driving all the way from Toronto with a small U-Haul van, and my parents drove from Virginia.

Today, my two closest friends, Laura and Becky, showed up to offer support. This is the day we are packing up my old apartment. Truly. It's been sold, and the new family is moving in this week.

My ex is staying at a friend's so my family and I can fully clean out the apartment before the new tenants arrive. There are a few boxes for me to go through, and I'm to leave what I don't want for Jon to look at or throw away. This is all part of our mediation agreement. I'm here to do my part, even though I feel like my legs are going to give out.

After three months of staying at Beth's calming apartment uptown, re-entering my old home is like walking into a vice grip. I really never wanted to be here again. When we walk in, I see a large pile of Jon's things right by the door, and my whole body goes hot. Our explicit agreement was he would have all of his things out by today to make room for our cleaning. I want to scream and yell. I want to rail and pound the walls, but in the moment of intense rage, I am not alone. My mother squeezes my hand with understanding, and my brother's body stands in the doorway ready to take action.

I only slept two hours last night. I honestly don't know what I am running on right now. Thank goodness they are here.

As I feel the presence of my family and friends, I take in Jon's things and recognize his action as passive-aggressive behavior. For all of our marriage, I would get this feeling that something was off and would feel it was somehow my fault. But now I see. I see the aggression in full view for what it is.

Clearly he is pissed about all of this in his own way. He's not the only one who is angry. Perhaps that is the one thing we can share right now, ironically.

My mother goes into organization mode and starts delegating tasks. Everything has to come out, everything has to be packed. I'm putting my things in storage tomorrow and then living at a friend's in Weehawken, NJ until my new apartment is ready in Astoria at the beginning of July.

On the floor in front of me by the large window overlooking 34th Avenue is a pile. "We thought you needed to go through this to decide what you are taking and what you are leaving for Jon," my mother softly mentions.

While the pile is not that large, it feels like a mountain as I lower my body to see our movie collection. As I touch each one, I am remembering popcorn and soda, chocolates and endless nights we both lined up with wide eyes in the dark, coming out of the theater aglow with the thrill of the story and discussing the incredible acting or the cinematography.

With shaking hands, I make two piles. What was one collection—something we grew and loved together—is now divided. From one pile to two.

Then I hear Laura say, "Hey, Nik, I think you need to go through this box."

I walk away from the two piles to see her standing over the box labeled 'Christmas decorations,' and as she's starting to walk away, I grab her and say, "Please stay with me."

My favorite time of year has always been from Halloween to New Year's. Just one fun celebration after another, and the one I always loved the most was Christmas. And no matter the size of our apartment, it was covered with glitter and glee. We would sit on the couch at night with all the other lights off and just stare at our four-foot fiber optic tree, in awe of the changing lights.

Red to green to blue to orange to yellow.

And among the branches, ornaments ranging from SpongeBob Squarepants to Star Wars. A whole month of joy, and one we shared. We both loved Christmas. We were children together tearing open gifts on Christmas morning and playing endless Christmas songs.

Children who now were growing up and leaving home, but not together.

When I wasn't getting pregnant last year and panicking that something was wrong with me, I also was feeling terrified by Jon's words. I felt like he was constantly talking about how things were going to change with having a family, and not in a way that he wanted. One night I unleashed all my anger and frustration after hearing one more time how scared he was, and I yelled at him, "It's time to GROW UP!"

I saw something break in him. His whole body seemed to sink. I went into the bedroom and slammed the door shut.

After about an hour, I came out and found him on the floor of our office with papers strewn all around him. He looked like a lost child who had no idea where his parents were, his eyes glassed over and rummaging through each paper quickly with his hands. I don't even know what he was looking for, but I had never seen him like this.

I was terrified.

He didn't talk to me for a day after that fight and I apologized, but my insides were chilled. I couldn't stop shaking. What had I witnessed? What had my anger created? I didn't even fully remember all that I had said. So many words had fired from my stomach like razors, so much that had been tied up inside.

"He took care of you until you asked him to grow up. You were Peter Pan and Wendy," my therapist stated. I stopped breathing when she said this, the truth hitting me square in the chest. It wasn't just his fear of having kids, I also waited because I wanted to be on Broadway. I put off starting a family too. We were children together, locked in our agreement until I didn't want to play anymore.

Now, holding his favorite Christmas ornaments—which he had left behind—I can't stop crying.

Laura holds me, and Becky comes to hug me from the other side.

I just let it come, all the grief.

Wave after wave as the opened box lays between us all.

ELEVATOR

"DUN DUN DUN DUN, dun dun dun," my brother and I sing in tandem as we load up the elevator with all my furniture. Whispering the theme to *Mission Impossible*, I am actually smiling.

Our secret mission at midnight, we waited until everyone in the building was asleep to avoid the co-op supervisor, who had come earlier in the day telling us we couldn't use the elevator to move things without prior permission. Apparently, Jon had neglected to tell him.

As the new family was coming in two days, we didn't have that time, so my brother decided we were going to just be sneaky.

My parents were fast asleep already, and Laura and Becky had left hours ago.

It was just my brother and me. I was exhausted but feeling encouraged.

We had packed everything.

I had survived the ornaments and movies.

We load up the U-Haul in the slight breeze of the June Saturday night, and it is mostly quiet on the streets.

Nothing in our way, he locks up the U-Haul, packed to the brim, and I hug him, "I love you, bro."

He was the last person in the family I told about my affair. I was so terrified he would be disappointed in me. Here he was, with two children and the perfect life up in Toronto. He had figured it out, and I had blown my marriage apart. And yet, when I did tell him, he just met me with love. It was his idea to drive down with a U-Haul.

My big brother, here.

We make our way up to the apartment, and I grab a few last things to put in my car. The backseat is full of clothes, my altar stuff, shoes, and many documents. These are all the things I will need for the next month, and all the rest will go into storage.

I look down at my backpack and decide to grab it. It does have my computer and valuables in it. Probably a good idea to keep with me in the apartment.

It's after 2 a.m., and I breathe in the night air. I'm feeling my heart open a little.

I crawl into bed with my brother on the pull-out sofa in the living room and actually feel some peace.

We did it.

We did it together.

Maybe things are going to be ok after all. Maybe there is some hope.

"See you in a few hours," I giggle to my brother.

Tomorrow I leave this place for good, and I can't wait. I am now ready to leave it behind.

HANGER

TODAY, I LEAVE THIS APARTMENT. I wake up after only a few hours of sleep, but I feel so hopeful. I smile at my brother and ask if I can go take a shower first.

"Go for it!" he smiles back at me.

I hop out of the pull-out sofa bed and take off all the sheets with my brother's help, knowing I will never sleep in this bed again. And that feels so amazing.

I take a gloriously hot shower and am humming as the water cascades down my skin, warming my body and refreshing my pores.

It's going to be a good day.

I'm drying myself off when I hear my mother outside the bathroom door, "Toots… can you come out here?"

I wrap the towel around me and open the door to see my mother almost rigid and frozen, as she looks at me and says, "Your car door is open, and everything is gone."

I feel my whole body stop for a moment, and in a flash, I play out going to my car at 2 a.m. Oh dear GOD… did I not lock the car??

And then I collapse on the floor in my towel, naked in front of my mother, father and brother and break apart.

"No, no, no, no, no, no" running out of my mouth in an endless stream.

My mother tries to pick me up off the floor, and urges me into my clothes so we can go out together and look. My heart is pounding.

So much was in my car; everything I need for the next month was in there.

And thoughts are flying through my head at lightning speed.

Did I lock the car?

Did someone watch me and wait to break in?

I thought I lived in a safe neighborhood!

How is this happening?!?

How is this happening?!?

I stumble down to my car on the street and see the backseat completely empty. My father and brother start running down the street to look in trash cans, to see if they can find anything.

And my mind starts to remember everything that was in there.

My clothes.

My shoes.

All my banking information.

My check book.

My altar pieces I had lovingly put together over these last three months.

My audition book of songs, fully curated after 18 years in the business.

My audition and dance clothes.

My dance shoes.

All my belts.

And all my underwear.

My brother returns with a hanger, stating, "I found this on the sidewalk. Is this yours?"

A single hanger, the only thing remaining.

And worst of all, I might have done this to myself. It was 2 in the morning. I may have forgotten to lock my own car with my most important possessions inside. What was in the car was all of who I was, all that was left.

I did this to myself.

Why would I do that?

I call Beth's husband, who works for the NYPD, to ask for help and start to file a report. I call my bank to say I need to put a freeze on my account and open a new one. I seem to be outside my body but forming words.

Then we call insurance, and they encourage me to write out a list of everything.

Everything...

I'm losing track at this point of all I've lost. I watch my mother sweep the apartment, and I look at the walls and floor of this home that held me for eight years—this home where I was certain we would have a family. I don't even register the goodbye because my whole body is in shock.

Somehow, as if in a daze, we take all my things to storage, and my family follows me to Weehawken, to my friend's place where I will be living with her and her husband for a month.

My family leaves, and I go into my new room, shutting the door.

It was supposed to be a good day. It was supposed to be a good day.

I don't understand. I don't understand.

The Friend comes into my body
looking for the center, unable
to find it, draws a blade,
strikes anywhere.

— Rumi

LAKE

I WAKE UP IN the new room.
I have to go to a temp job.

I have to call insurance.

I have to follow up with the bank.

I have to take a shower and eat.

I roll out onto the floor beside the bed to meditate, realizing I don't have any of my altar pieces. Considering how much I cried yesterday, no tears come now. Just a heavy acknowledgment of the nightmare before me.

Ok, I'll just sit here, facing the corner.

I start to meditate and see a black lake in front of me. I feel myself drawn towards it, like a magnet.

Standing on the shore, I peek down into the dark waters, thick like ink.

For a moment, I imagine myself walking down into the water, and just disappearing forever.

I wouldn't have to deal with anything there.

I could just escape there.

I would be safe there.

The water is right next to my toes, and then something even stronger pulls me away from the water's edge.

The lake disappears.

I take a shower and decide that, today, I am going to buy myself some underwear.

Jon bought me all of those that were in the backseat anyway. Maybe it's a good thing I don't have them anymore.

Gratitude/Victories List
6/6/13

- Temped
- Meditated
- Opened savings account
- Saw therapist
- Grateful for my parents, brother, friends, this bedroom, Buddhism, my aunt giving me a box full of belts
- Grateful for my friend giving me a bag full of her old clothes

POSTER

COMING OUT OF YOGA CLASS for the first time since the robbery, I can feel myself breathing.

I've found some great sales, and my friends are offering clothes to me. I'm on a long-term temp job assignment that is saving my life. Having somewhere to go every day with a time structure is really helping, plus keeping an income flowing.

I feel like I walk in constant fear of running into my ex on the street. Everywhere I look, I see our memories, and I'm still having night sweats and pain in my chest. I would love to get away. Far away.

Looking up on the studio wall, I see a poster for a yoga retreat to Guatemala.

It's next month, and it's over my birthday.

I immediately go to the front desk and sign up.

I've never been on a yoga retreat before.

I've never been on ANY kind of retreat before.

I've never been to Guatemala.

And I've never gone through a devastating divorce, lost my home, and been robbed all within the span of six months.

Everything is new.

NEIGHBORS

MY MOM AND I SPENT WEEKS playing with a large sheet of gridded paper and tiny cut-outs of furniture to see how we could fit everything into my new 300 square-foot apartment.

This apartment came so easily as a friend of mine lives next door and told me about it months ago. I was terrified to be paying so much per month, the most I ever had in the city, but with my temp jobs and a new freelance office organization job, the universe seemed to be supplying me with what I needed. It felt comforting to know my friend was literally a wall away. The apartment is in a house that has been converted into four units. Two on the first floor/below street level, one on the second and one on the third. A house, not a large co-op building like I lived in for the last eight years where I barely knew any of my neighbors.

I'm 37, and I've never lived by myself. I went straight from my parents' house to college with roommates, and then was married two weeks after I graduated from college.

It is hands down the smallest bathroom I have ever been in. You step out of the shower directly into the sink and with one step are then sitting on the toilet.

Today is move-in day, the beginning of living here, and my parents have arrived as support to make the grid a reality. I am overcome with gratitude for their continued presence and care.

Around lunch, my neighbors from the third floor knock on the door to introduce themselves and invite us to their July 4th BBQ in the backyard.

The backyard.

I've never had that in the whole 15 years I have lived in New York City. I've seen some friends who had them and always thought how incredible that would be, and here I was moving into a new place that actually had one.

My parents and I walk out back to a festive gathering of people. I stand still in shyness for a moment, and my neighbors see me, coming right up with open, smiling faces. Leading me through the yard, they introduce me to each of their friends, one at a time. I feel so welcomed, and the sun is warming my face. This feels miraculous.

Shaking hands, meeting a new community, enjoying some food together.

My first apartment in Astoria where my ex and I lived was really wonderful for the first three years, and we did know our neighbors below and above us. But, then the elderly woman who lived above us moved into a home and everything changed. The new group of neighbors didn't put down a stitch of carpet, and would have gatherings around the equinox and moon cycles, staying up late. All we would hear was a high-pitched "ooooooooooo," some giggling, and then furniture being moved around. And this would repeat over and over.

We could never make sense of what they were doing, and it was the first time I had to start sleeping with earplugs. I tried talking with them, asking first politely if they could put down some carpet and keep the noise down. This simply didn't work, even though I received nods and apologies. So, things got ugly. Really ugly. Nothing I tried was creating quiet. I threatened to call the cops on them and wrote a hateful letter saying I was going to be taking legal action.

I called the city for help, and they directed me back to the superintendent. Well, the super lived beneath us, except he died of cancer, and the wife took over the building. The timing was awful. She had no interest in keeping the peace. And then she passed away too, leaving the building in the hands of her daughter with the loss of both parents. I never asked for her help. That first apartment began as a place of quiet, where the only noise was really when my ex and I were fighting, and then the noise seemed to be all around me. I was angry all the time.

So, we took the grand step of buying a co-op with the help of my parents and moved in with stars in our eyes. We both loved the apartment so much, and the new neighborhood out in Jackson Heights. It had great flow, lots of natural light, and being in a co-op meant there would actually be rules to protect us with any neighbor issues. The two times we went to see the apartment before we moved in, it was so quiet, I was convinced there must be cement between the floors.

This apartment would be different. It would be peaceful. It would be quiet. I would be less angry.

And then the very first night we spent there, my ex came down with the flu, the toilet broke, and all we heard were children running like crazy above our heads and conversations clear as day. This began a six-month battle with the family upstairs who had no carpet and was actually trying to illegally erect a wall so more family members could move in.

I went from fighting to fighting.

Fighting to fighting with my neighbors, becoming more and more angry, and it drained me completely.

I was tired of fighting. Exhausted really. There had to be another way. I had just spent three months up at Beth's apartment, which was so quiet, and the neighbors were so lovely. I knew it existed, I just didn't know how to create it for myself in the face of conflict.

———————————

As I meet my neighbors in our shared backyard, I feel a spark of hope. Could I finally experience real quiet here? Not just quiet around me, but quiet inside myself?

I head inside feeling inspired, ready to finish setting up the furniture with my parents. I feel my body start to relax as I look at what they brought up for me. It was actually a few pieces that belonged to my grandmother. She lived with my parents the last year and a half of her life, before passing two years ago.

I feel her there with me and am grateful.

I didn't want to take any of the old furniture from my other apartment, but I couldn't afford to buy new. My grandmother's furniture actually seemed to balance out the energy of the other pieces. Her desk was now positioned next to the bookshelf my former father-in-law made. Her small table stood with strength next to the kitchen cart I bought with my ex eight years ago.

I miss my grandma.

A year before she passed, she came to see me and my ex in a musical we were performing in. Sitting outside the restaurant waiting on the rest of our family, she looked me right in the eyes and said, "Don't wait too long to have kids." I was terrified at the time, feeling so frustrated in my career and still pining for my dream to be on Broadway. I was also in a show where my character was cheated on by her husband. And my husband was playing my husband in the show. It was a complete mind fuck. I had kept my affair a secret and was promising myself I was never going to call Dan again, and felt like the show was the universe pointing a big finger at me. Maybe this was punishment. And Jon was feeling so distant. I injured myself in the show, twisting my ankle during dress rehearsal, and he barely responded. I was fighting with the artistic director over contract issues, and Jon wasn't standing up for me. And I just thought, "I deserve this."

Looking into my grandmother's concerned face, I imagined telling her I was pregnant and how proud of me she would be, but I wasn't ready to get off the pill that summer. And then, at the beginning of 2011, my last words to her were a poem spoken from the pulpit for her funeral service.

She left my ex and I her car, but it was in my name, so in the separation, I took it. I had never driven in the city before and found myself behind the wheel on city streets for the first time in my life. I thought I would be a horrible driver. Jon constantly criticized my driving and we always fought when I was behind the wheel. I thought I would be terrified with all the traffic and high energy. Instead, I drove with ease. Much like holding the tarantula, I proved to myself I could do something scary. I actually could do it really well, and a fear that I had been carrying around for years disappeared when I turned the ignition.

Thank you, Grandma. I feel you here.

Outside in the hallway, my mother has a box open and asks, "This is your wedding stuff. Where do you want it?"

"Can you keep that back at your house, Mom? I really want to watch what I bring into this apartment."

We nod at each other, and she tapes the box back up without me even looking in it. I know that it won't be healthy for me to see the contents now. I have a lot of healing to do.

Maybe here I can do that.

Here with neighbors who I know. Here with neighbors I'm not fighting with. Or maybe it's just me choosing not to fight anymore. I seemed to be fighting everyone before my divorce, and it never worked.

If I'm not fighting, then what am I doing?

PHOENIX

SETTLING IN IS PROVING HARDER than I hoped. I feel strange here. I feel lonely here, and constantly confused by the pieces of furniture that were bought with a vision of a life together.

And I've got to clean out my computer. I actually went onto social media and deleted all the photos that had Jon in them and blocked him. While it was necessary, it felt like I had opened the wound back up and poured salt on, rubbing it in with painful vigor. My dear friend Stacy, who is a tech wiz, helped me to pick out an external hard drive so I would have all the information that was on the shared drive from my marriage. Except when I got it back after mediation, it didn't have all my photos on it. Years worth of photos gone... and I was resolute to not reach out to Jon. I received the hard drive months ago, just didn't have the emotional capacity to look at it, until now.

Except it appears I don't have the capacity now either.

The apartment doesn't feel like my home. It feels like a stranger.

I'm making the trek every Sunday to Zen service in Brooklyn from Queens and finding great solace there. I don't speak to anyone really, but I feel safe there. Sitting in meditation with a group feels like a refuge. And the Abbott of the temple has become a shining beacon. His talks go right through me, as if he is speaking directly to me.

Last week, he spoke of the walls we create in our minds and offered the invitation to stand in front of the wall and take it down piece by piece. This felt like such a relief, and as I sat in meditation, I saw the image of removing one stone at a time carefully, my hands gingerly removing a heavy, rounded mass. As I stared at the gray matter, I knew this

13

first stone was my mind. Beginning with the step of having a daily meditation practice, I had tools around the thoughts and beliefs that had driven my life for years for the first time.

As my therapy continues, I am really beginning to see there was a lot that led up to the divorce. There is a lot unraveling within me and actually coming to light. This isn't about smashing a wall to pieces in one swoop; this is going to be a process. Smashing the wall feels horrible anyway. I tried that for years. It never worked.

And I have no idea how long it will take to dismantle the wall. Some days I'm ok with that, although most days I really struggle with the enormity of it and desperately want it to go faster. This hurts. A lot.

While I feel too shy to speak to the other practitioners who come weekly to Zen service, I feel safe to speak to the Abbott and share with him where I am and what brought me to Zen and my profound experience at the intro to Zen Training weekend. He always makes space for me, taking me in with his big, calm eyes and offering words of support.

I'm learning about impermanence and Buddha nature. Both of these feel like a healing balm to me. I had created a belief that not only could I control things, but that things were permanent, non-changing. And now, with the help of Zen, I am really seeing how this is causing me and has caused me so much suffering in my career and my marriage. Realizing that impermanence is actually the root of reality changes everything. One, it means that my marriage ending was actually ok. It was never permanent, and also that the state I am in now will change.

I can change.

This coupled with the teaching that I possess Buddha nature, that I am whole and complete as I am, is crucial. I feel such deep shame for my affair, and now feel hope that I can heal this, and also that I am not a "bad" person at my core. I am not the sinner I was taught I was in Sunday school. I was actually horribly unhappy and terribly confused. I created massive damage with my actions, and I can atone because I am whole.

Atone = at one.

This is becoming my foundation and keeps me motivated to continue to meditate every day, to go to therapy, and become a student of Zen.

After moving into my apartment, I updated the Abbott on where I was, and he said, "It's as if you are in the same room you were always in, but now the lights are on."

Yes.

This is my life. This is my being and body. And I was so disconnected. I had no idea how to help myself, how to ask for help, and yet, when I lost everything and did ask for help, it came, and it's coming. Day after day, I am being surrounded by care. My friends, my family, new teachers, all leading me back to looking within.

As I took in the Abbott's words, I suddenly realized I don't know where the light switch is anymore. I actually couldn't turn the lights off in my room again, even if I tried. In losing everything, I've lost the ability. The light is on. And it's bright, and it's blinding, and I have a lot to look at. But for the first time in my life, I want to. In fact, I now realize if I want a different life than the one I had, I have to keep the lights on, regardless of what I discover. Regardless of how ugly it appears at first.

Another teaching that has been really hitting home has been the concept of my ego burning to ash. Except in the wake of the robbery, I feel like my life is burning to ash. I know things need to change, but how much fire is in front of me? How much has to burn?

How long is this going to take?

Am I safe now in this apartment?

Or is this just the beginning of much more that has to fall away?

Feeling vulnerable, I call Stacy after looking at my closed computer and deciding there's no way I can clean it out today.

Unloading where I am, I say to her, "I feel like I'm burning to ash, again and again."

There's a beat of silence, and she says, "You're a phoenix." And then she texts me a picture of the X-Men character Jean Gray, standing strong, with flame leaping off her body.

And just like that moment at the Zen Training weekend when I was asked if I was ok without Jon, something changes.

The phoenix rises. No matter how many times it burns, the Phoenix always rises. I realized I had been placing all my attention on the fact that I was burning down, and Stacy helped me reframe it to focus on the fact that I was rising every time.

Rising from the divorce.

Rising from the affair.

Rising from the robbery.

I can rise.

Oh, thank you, Stacy. Thank you, thank you, thank you.

No matter what comes, I can rise.

STEP 4
PITI

Rapture

Travel Journal Entry
7/20/13

I'm in Guatemala… I'm in a luxurious room by myself, snuggled under a down comforter, hearing the laughter of our group outside along with the light patter of rain. Today began with my alarm going off at 2:15 a.m. for a 2:30 a.m. cab to the airport. Six out of the 13 retreaters flew together through San Salvador and took a 3-hour van ride to take a 15 minute boat trip to arrive here in paradise. To enjoy gigantic smoothies, organic tea, an absolutely lush microcosm of a center facing two volcanoes. I shared my story with mostly everyone.

And I feel a deep quiet here. No songs on repeat running through my head, no protective wall… just beauty and nature and air, and a group of people seeking something in their lives.

Here I am, seeking peace, seeking refuge, and I feel a relaxation that is new.

There is a spider on my wall, a "wallie" as Sharon, our host, called them. I feel no need to kill it, or get rid of it. I actually like having it in the room with me… my fear on the wall while I sleep.

I'm so glad I have my own room, and I'm reveling in the space.

There is a Buddha on my balcony, a spider on my wall, and a yoga studio above me. I'm in heaven. I'm in Guatemala.

Travel Journal Entry
7/21/13

I woke at 4 a.m. today to pitch black, the power being out, and a beautiful lightning storm over the lake. I grabbed my flashlight to check all the switches and for a moment was overwhelmed by the darkness and quiet. I felt a fear, and then I fell back asleep.

When my alarm went off, I didn't want to get up. I was cozy but rose to squeeze in 10 minutes of meditation before the 7:30 class. It was chilly outside, but my view as I rolled out my mat in the yoga studio was the volcano. It felt unreal, magical, and intense to be practicing in front of such a giant of nature. The teacher had us contemplate a few words, "nature, survival, destruction, family, ancestors." My flesh raised with "survival." It has been my strongest intention through this process and pain. "Destruction" also resonated: the destruction of my marriage, my trust, our shared love and life… my ego, my attachment, my plans… I could feel a good and bad association. I was tight from traveling and the class was more basic, but it felt wonderful, and I released tears as we said our final "om." I felt a letting go and acceptance of the words that rang so true in my body.

We had a delicious breakfast and then gathered at the dock for our day trip to Santiago. It was about a 20-30 minute boat ride and the sun was shining, bringing much warmer temps than the early morning. I snapped several photos of Volcano San Pedro in excitement for Wednesday and the hike to the top. I realized I was looking forward to the trip and not having to convince my ex as I had so many times in our marriage. This moment is mine alone.

We pulled into Santiago and met Dolores, our Mayan tour guide. The docks were the beginning of a long stretch of vendors and stores filled with local crafts. Dolores wisely advised us to wait until after the tour to shop.

Dolores was a presence, a calm spiritual educator. She had actually married an American and lived in Arizona and New Mexico for 10 years before deciding to come back home to Santiago, remarry, and become a tour guide and spiritual advisor. She speaks Mayan, Spanish, and English, and fled Guatemala at the beginning of their civil war in the early 1980s. She had to hide out for 6 months before going to the US. She acts as an advisor to natural spiritual healers who have not honored their calling and become physically sick due to this. She encourages them to follow the spiritual gifts they were given and said when they do, they feel better. This was amazing to me as I think of my cough and so many ways my grief has manifested itself in my body… and yet, I have not really been sick.

Sometimes I think the shame and secret of my affair was an illness in me, my disappointments in my ex an illness in me… now gone.

Dolores took us to a shrine for Maximon, a Mayan and Catholic saint-figure who locals travel to receive blessings and protection from. A family had traveled from Guatemala City for a ceremony with the medicine man, and we witnessed them all, on the mats, kneeling, offering liquor, cigarettes, and cigars. The medicine man took a hat with a scarf attached to the brim, placing it on each of their heads, forward and backwards, placing blessings of protection. At the same time, another ceremony was going on for St. Francis, the protector of animals, and a family had come back to give gratitude for the blessings they had received on their business. It was incredible witnessing the ceremonies, the faith of the participants, and hearing the medicine man's incantations.

We walked through a bustling marketplace full of food and made our way to a Catholic/Mayan church built 500 years ago. From the church, we ended up at Dolores's parents' house to witness traditional Mayan weaving. Her mother sat on a mat on the ground, weaving while Dolores explained the process. There was embroidery Dolores had done and many scarves and tortilla covers her mother had made. Many of us purchased these items, and my eye went to a beautiful embroidery of Guatemalan birds. As my parents are huge bird lovers, I paid for the beautiful artwork with the plan to gift it at Christmas as a thank you for all the support they have given me this year.

We ended our time by shopping along the main street and enjoying our incredible packed lunch. Every meal I've had has been incredible. It's all vegetarian and reminds me of the incredible cooking from the monastery.

Travel Journal Entry
7/22/13

Shiva slept in my room. I wanted her to come, and after mewing outside another room, she made her way to mine and was all too happy to curl up in my crotch and wash herself endlessly. It was an interesting night of sleep. She would always find the crook of my legs on top of the blankets so I would feel like I couldn't move. Once she finished cleaning herself, I fell asleep and was woken in the middle of the night to a terrible sound, like a beast being killed. Shiva was unfazed and just resituated herself. No one else in our group heard it. Part of me wonders if it was a dream, but it's so clear to me, and I remember waking up. I fell back asleep to be woken up by the chickens at 6 a.m. making a crazy ruckus. I then fell into a very deep, short sleep where I dreamt I let a piglet into the room who slept with Shiva and I. I also dreamt my alarm went off, and Shiva spoke to me saying, "Thank goodness you set your alarm early. None of the others do." My alarm then really went off, and I thought Shiva would want out, but she stayed in, being frisky, and chasing her tail as I was meditating. As I wasn't giving her attention, she started to meow at me, so I let her out right before the gong sounded for yoga.

The morning class was all about water and was wonderful. It was nice to have the music back in the flow, as yesterday both teachers opted for silence.

After another incredible meal, those of us who opted out of doing a hike put on our suits and settled in by the pool. Some took a dip in Lake Atitlan, but I stayed cautious on the dock, so concerned the water would make me sick. They all emerged so refreshed, and the sun was hot, so I decided to lower myself in... it was powerful... the current was so strong, and I felt an endless depth beneath me. The temp was so refreshing, and Diana snapped some photos of me. I emerged shaking and exhausted. I felt like I had swum several laps, and I had only treaded water for a minute or two. My legs were shaking...

What just happened? Did the lake take something from me?

I took a long hot shower and went upstairs to the other yoga studio to meditate for 30 minutes. I experienced super sleepy zazen, but the space was breathtaking. What a gift to sit in front of the yoga altar in such a sacred and beautiful space all alone. I came back to my room and crashed for a half hour.

The evening yoga class began with the mantra, "sa ta na ma"… I had a real circular moment, remembering my search for a mantra I could repeat, some vocal power to gain inspiration in Salt Lake as I was drowning in non-acceptance of my reality. I remember the yellow Post-it note I kept by my yoga mat in the apartment I was staying in, as a reminder of the phases of life.

Tonight, the teacher gave us all bolsters at the end of class to lay on, opening our upper bodies, and I became very aware of my heartbeat in my back, then of the tightness around my heart… and then I was weeping and couldn't stop. I felt I was saying goodbye to Jon and worried I wouldn't be able to stop crying… then I said, "This too," and allowed the tears instead of holding them back. I let the waves come through the final forward bends, wiping my face and nose as the flow continued. In savasana, the tears dried. The sadness I was sitting in passed, but there was a letting go. This was a reminder I'm not on vacation… I'm on a healing retreat, and though it may become intense, I'm safe here. They know my story. We all shared dinner after, and I was feeling as though I had passed through something.

This group is special. It's such a mix of people, but the commitment to yoga is a great denominator.

My "wally" is now hanging out on the curtain, and though I experience some goosebumps when I look at him, I feel grateful he's here. I'm sleeping with fear… and it's lessening. I'm having a curiosity with spiders now I never thought possible. There is a destruction happening, of so many preconceived ideas and plans, of my shock that I'm a divorcee, and yet I still feel it.

I'm so glad I opted for my own room. Coming to peace with solitude.

Travel Journal Entry
7/23/13

It's almost 2 p.m., and I became so overwhelmed, so rocked to the core by the Mayan Shaman, Thomas's reading, I asked Diana to bring me food to my room. I became open, vulnerable, couldn't stop the tears… collapsed on my floor to fully allow the break within. I'm sitting on the floor now looking at the volcano, hearing the happy lunch sounds of our group, knowing I needed solitude. I needed to process…

I wrote my name, time of birth, and birthdate on a white scrap of paper, and on the backside, Thomas wrote my chart, consulting his book and counting on his fingers at each step. A gentle, young face, he thanked me first for allowing him to do this. He spoke of a path and direction, and I started to weep.

He said I loved too much, which went to my depths, echoing Jon's words to me in Salt Lake.

He spoke of finding balance, which has truly been my desire, but I have had to dive and wade through so much.

He spoke of how hard I am on myself and how that, in turn, makes me hard on others. This also went to my core, remembering the judgments and disappointments I felt in Jon, in myself for my affair and destructive behavior, in so many angry words I threw not understanding the origin.

He said I had so much fire behind me, and I need to let it consume me to move forward, to help others, and see their individuality.

He saw insecurity, pain, physical pain, and spoke of not being able to accomplish certain things because of this insecurity. I thought of my choreography, my poetry, my need and deep desire to create, and how I have felt unsuccessful and thwarted.

He warned me of ambition and pride.

He also said I need to be a vibrant color... I loved this. I've never been a wallflower.

And then he surprised me saying the number 11 in the middle of my chart spoke of a call to heal. He inquired if I had ever wanted to be a doctor, and I thought of my desire in my 20s to be a massage therapist or my recent thought to form a divorce support group. I have always wanted to help people, loved nurturing children, teaching... and Thomas said I will probably write a book of healing later in life... could this be the story I am living now? A collection of short stories or poems?

He also said to surround myself with ancient things to help balance and to burn incense. I shared about my grandparents' furniture and smiled thinking how much I have enjoyed burning incense daily as I meditate.

He said I have good dreams, strong dreams, and to trust in them… I thought of all I have seen in my sleep over these past 8 months, and of the dreams that inspired poetry.

So many Hafiz poems spoke of burning to ash in order to see God, to find God, to truly find love… how I wished at times I would be consumed, and yet all along, I feel there has been a destruction.

Ground myself…

Balance…

Fire

Fire

Fire

He said there is a great opportunity here, in this place.

Trust

Heal

See

Part 2
7/23/13

I am practically in a zombie state, and it's just before 9 p.m., but I let go of so much today, I am beyond exhausted. I've enjoyed a lovely shower and want to write a little about the fire protection ceremony today because it was one of the most powerful spiritual experiences I've ever had.

The ceremony lasted over two hours and was on a small patch of grass right by the thin boardwalk, with the lake water churning and rain falling intermittently.

Thomas first built an elaborate fire with resin, wood, a circle with a cross of sugar (symbolizing life), candy, candles, rosemary.. it was endless, and as Thomas got to each energy, we counted to 13 in Mayan and gave an offering. The smoke of the fire felt amazing as it washed over me. When Thomas first lit the fire and started chanting very quickly in his native tongue, I began to weep. The power, the palpable energy... He said so many beautiful things about love, life, the power of nature, and so much resonated with me.

The fire spoke to him, and a bee floated by to pass along the importance of each other. Thomas blessed our feet, placing his hands, warmed by the fire, onto both, then left, then right. I felt grounded, I felt firm.

He spoke of the feminine energy and how this year in the Mayan calendar was a good opportunity for change. I shivered as the wind picked up but was mesmerized and moved, not just by Thomas, but by our group, our communal moment and dedication.

We walked in a circle, chanting; we held hands, and many cried. I made an offering for balance and spoke of my desire to let go... to say, "I could not have changed Jon's mind." To stop beating myself up over Dan, and left it in the fire.

We all picked a flower or plant and whispered our past... I asked the purple thistle to remember the sacred and beautiful love that did exist, and then threw it into the lake for the lake to remember... my past.

Though Thomas said he is only a humble medicine man, he was a conduit and a miracle today.

Time to dream... I'll write more later.

Travel Journal Entry
7/24/13

I sit in the afternoon shade by the pool, looking at the majestic volcano (San Pedro) I had planned to and deeply desired to climb today. I am exhausted, spent, empty, from a night on the toilet. What began with cramping and some big bowel movements then became waking up hot and having diarrhea.

I prayed this would pass. I knew what it meant, that I would be weakened beyond a state to hike, or really do much… and here I am with a very unhappy belly, nibbling on rice sticks and drinking the "bad belly" tea..

I feel the lesson Thomas spoke of with not being so hard on myself, but surrounded by such beauty and feeling so crappy, it is a challenge.

I know yesterday was total overwhelm and, in truth, I'm ready for that to lessen. My head is light with lack of food, and my belly still churns. I am sick of everything, sick of all these suppositions, theories… the reality remains, and still hurts. How I wish to truly sleep. Rest, and wake refreshed and stronger. I continue to empty when I think no more bottom exists. Is this the moment of gratitude? That I am able— and have come to a place that allows—such letting go? I'm going to close my eyes and come back to write.

After a nap, I immediately grabbed my phone to chronicle my dream. It was the first time Jon was kind to me… we were kissing, he was carrying an old woman's luggage, and a friend was singing how she still had faith. It felt like reconciliation, but not the kind between us, but within me. A peace, where he wasn't morphing into a snake, crumbling with a broken neck, fighting with me again and again… but carrying luggage. It seems no small coincidence that this occurred today after my emotional and physical purge.

I reached for the breakfast tortillas, which smelled good now, whereas earlier they repulsed me. I nibbled though one and a half and felt feverish. I heard the dinner bell, and though I didn't want to go, I knew I needed food and possibly a thermometer. I was light-headed. I ended up running into Sharon, the owner, who took such good care of me, finding a thermometer, and recounting her sickness from last year. She then made me homemade gatorade, an absolute lifesaver. I had laid in bed hoping for pasta or potatoes, and there was plain pasta. What a gift. Sharon got me butter for my bread, and I sat down with everyone.

It was a quiet group as the volcano hike proved to be very challenging. People were exhausted. I sat in between two of the teachers, and one understood my desire to hike the volcano. He had opted out as well because he didn't have proper shoes. He simply stated it wasn't his time, and I realized I didn't come to this retreat to hike a volcano, I came to heal.

Maybe the Mayan reading and Fire ceremony was my volcano, my late night purge my challenge. I am physically strong, but it's the emotional strength that I seek, that I've been working on.

After dinner, and finding out my temperature was below normal, I walked down the stone steps and looked up to a sea of stars… breathtaking.

Someone earlier in the week had said they don't really get that here and three nights ago, we had a full bright moon. I found a table to lie on, and felt such deep gratitude staring at the centered cluster. I saw two shooting stars and started to understand true self-love.

I am feeling better.

Travel Journal Entry
7/25/13

My birthday :). I woke at 5:15 a.m. from a glorious sleep feeling so much better, and watched the sunrise from my balcony, eating what was left of my second tortilla. After realizing my piece of bread had been taken over by the ants, I put in earplugs and fell into a deep sleep of vivid dreams about being late for yoga and having to go through school corridors. The alarm went off at 7, I felt good, and decided to try morning class.

Everyone wished me Happy Birthday, and I learned others had a rough night. The volcano hike had been a lot, and we were nearing the end of the week. I stayed in the back of the class, but was able to do much more than I expected and felt such bliss and gratitude. I was feeling self-love and a lack of anger. It was divine. At the end of class, one of the teachers read a poem about elephants and I cried, as it spoke of keeping your memories clean… and then everyone sang to me. Tears of gratitude poured. It was so sweet, so heartfelt and genuine.

After a small breakfast of toast and butter, I had my massage with Elaine. I ended up sharing all my details with her, even my affair. It felt right, in the space of intimate healing. Elaine was a divorcee too, and even though she said she didn't usually talk during massages, she shared her story with me about marrying a dancer who was controlling, so she divorced after two years. She shared how her body wouldn't get pregnant either because she knew it was wrong. She's been remarried for 23 years, but it's been a challenge, and she actually opted out of having kids because she didn't think the marriage would survive. She's 53 now and grateful to be past the point where people expected her to have kids.

I was worried the massage would loosen things in a bad way, but it did the opposite, and my cramps actually subsided. Her strokes and kneading were amazing. We were in a healing hut by the lake, and the sounds of the water lapping was so peaceful. At the end, she gave me a rigorous scalp massage and then balanced my chakras. As she began at the top of my head, all I saw with my eyes closed were circles stacked up in a line. Then, as she touched my throat, I began to cry, and it felt like everything was vibrating, and I felt Elaine shaking. She made her way down and placed her hands over my vagina, and I felt such warmth, I knew she was sending good energy for me to have children. I would have believed it if she somehow impregnated me on the spot!

She ended with my feet and then choked out a "thank you." I knew she had experienced something too. I put on my clothes and came outside, giving her the deepest hug, asking what just happened. She said there was so much energy radiating through my throat chakra that she had to contain it only to her arms. If she had allowed herself to take it all in, she wouldn't have been able to do her other massages. She then said my heart chakra blossomed, and she had given me blessings over my womb. She said I was exactly what she needed today, as the last words she had spoken to her husband that morning were "fuck you." How incredible I helped her as she was healing me so beautifully. I thought of Thomas's words, and this was proof to my central energy. What was nice was owning it.

After lunch, I was able to talk to my parents, as they called the office phone. I couldn't really start filling them in on all the details, because I was in the courtyard, but it was so lovely to talk to them. My mother's energy reminded me of the world awaiting me, and I began to understand other retreaters' concerns about re-entering the world. What a magic and power here... now, the challenge lies in moving forward, in taking this back to that small apartment and filling it with the same love.

I spent time on social media, loving all the messages and texts. So many reached out today, and though a part of me wanted the annual Dan text or thought I would get a "nice guy" message from Jon, neither reached out. That's huge. Maybe they are both angry at me, but there was also a relief that in this newfound joy, nothing was marring my day. This is a new beginning, a new year, and I am free of them both. Laura had emailed me saying she thought it would be a day of mixed emotions... and I realized that, for the first time, it wasn't! There was no sadness that I wasn't spending this day with Jon. There was no longing. What a miracle. The day belongs to me again.

Evening yoga was more restorative, and the teacher spoke about heart transplant patients taking on the likes and dislikes of their donors. Proof positive of the connection between love and the physical heart. I felt stronger in the night class and had realized earlier in the afternoon how calm the lake was. It was the first day we didn't see it churning up as the day progressed.

I went for a dip around 4 and felt this phenomenon. I was connected to the lake. The waters reflected my inner calm. Another birthday gift.

The staff presented me with a birthday cake, and the group gave me the most beautiful card with an elephant on a tightrope. I told them how amazing this was because of the elephant poem today and Ganesha being such an inspiration in my yoga practice this year.

My system is still normalizing, but I feel so much better. What a difference in energy from yesterday.

I gazed at the beautiful stars after dinner and felt such gratitude.

This was a birthday unlike any other. I received a gift more precious than any material thing and had so many moments today of smiling to myself. I feel the change, I feel the self love, and I feel the opening, the possibility of a different future, and coming to peace with all the pain I have endured. Jon not reaching out today was a door closed… the last one, and I needed that too.

I dressed in my new white dress for dinner. The choice was no mistake.

Now, I begin…

Washing the Elephant

*Isn't it always the heart that wants to wash
the elephant, begging the body to do it
with soap and water, a ladder, hands,
in tree-shade big enough for the vast savannahs
of your sadness, the strangler fig of your guilt,
the cratered full moon's light fueling
the windy spooling memory of elephant?*

*It takes more than half a century to figure out who they were,
the few real loves-of-your-life and how much of the rest—
the mad breaking-heart stickiness—falls away, slowly,
unnoticed, the way you lose your taste for things
like Popsicles unthinkingly.
And though dailiness may have no place
for the ones that have etched themselves in the laugh lines
and frown lines on the face that's harder and harder
to claim as your own, often one love-of-your-life
will appear in a dream, arriving
with the weight and certitude of an elephant,
and it's always the heart that wants to go out and wash
the huge mysteriousness of what they meant, those memories
that have only memories to feed them, and only you to keep them clean.*

— Barbara Ras

Travel Journal Entry
7/26/13

Last day in Guatemala.

I woke up, wrote down my dream, and did some bird watching, seeing a hummingbird.

All the stops were pulled out for morning class, and I was ready! I had more space in my upper back from the massage and was so grateful and happy to be feeling my strength again.

After breakfast, a group of us took a boat to Panahachel, across the lake. We all stopped to have a young coconut, and at first I wanted to pass as it just brought back memories of my own honeymoon, but then everyone was enjoying them so much, I chugged it down. My stomach cramped a little, but it really refreshed me and actually aided with the hot sun.

We then went to a 16th century church, and as soon as I entered, I was drawn to pray. I walked to the front and knelt, thanking God for all he has done, for his presence. Tears fell. I felt such gratitude. Behind me, in the open aisle, a family of three was kneeling, moving forwards and backwards, praying out loud, and the man held candles and offerings in his open hands. Their energy was palpable behind me, and I allowed the heat of their passion to wash over me and experience the moment. It was very powerful.

We hit the main shopping drag, and I found so many great gifts for friends and family, and this beautiful oil painting of a Guatemalan woman blossoming. I had sought art in Santiago to no avail. Nothing had been truly right to me… but this was. Now I can form my own art collection, which has always been a desire.

We returned for lunch, and Sharon came out to give us the check-out details. She said we were the first group she had checked in and out and was going to miss us. She took amazing care of us, as the owner is away (Sharon is the bookkeeper), and I will be forever indebted to her homemade gatorade.

Sitting out on the pier, another woman from our group shared her story of her marriage, her frustrations with her husband, and her inability to get past his infidelity she found out about around Christmas. They've only been married four years, and most of it unhappily... my heart bled for her as I saw her massive fear of change, and also clear unhappiness. I would never wish divorce on any couple, or person, as it's an awful process, but I also hear a lot of pain and denial. She came on this retreat to get away, but her anger is still deep. In some ways, I wonder how couples do stay together so long. They really do need to grow together.

I was touched she sought me out. I don't know if my words helped her, as she had so many questions about my journey. Sometimes I felt she was listening and at others she was skimming ahead. I do feel a fatigue with the story. It pains me to re-live. I'm feeling a shift in wanting to take that energy and place it elsewhere. I've needed to share it, a lot... and I know I will continue, but I feel an opening to other things, and that is a beautiful relief.

After an amazing last restorative yoga class, I hugged both the teachers and thanked them for all the incredible classes. They took such great care of us.

Dinner was jovial, and we exchanged addresses and phone numbers. The bugs seemed to be coming out to say farewell! A giant grasshopper landed on one of the teacher's pants, and we all gawked and took pictures. A huge moth flew in and made a quiet nest on the thatched ceiling.

I came back to my room to see Shiva here, and she is curled up so peacefully on my duvet. She is one of the coolest cats I have ever met. I feel a connection with her and am grateful for her presence tonight.

I'm all packed, have taken my shower, and it's nearing midnight. I feel time has passed here, and as we all said our goodbyes, a shift had occurred for us to move forward.

We shared something very sacred and special here, all 13 of us, and there was a common trust.

My last night in this room. It has been a sanctuary to sleep in, truly.

Travel Journal Entry
7/27/13

I'm on a full plane to JFK, it's almost midnight ET, and I feel such a panic in my stomach. I was ok to leave today, and grateful to have an extra two hours in the sun relaxing before catching the boat to Pana at noon. I've been exhausted since the traveling began. I conked out on the first short flight from Guatemala City to San Salvador, and now just feel so overwhelmed by the coughing children, my fatigue, and my empty tiny apartment awaiting me in a few hours. I found such peace in Guatemala. Will I be able to bring this forward into my life? I became so annoyed with the security at San Salvador airport, challenging them as they confiscated my water bottle. I felt the week slipping away and suddenly so aware of conflict all around. My security, my safety… it feels so far away, especially as I listen to a child in the seat behind me coughing over and over.

I had a true break this week and true breakthroughs. I took one last dip in Lake Atitlan today and was overcome as the cool, refreshing water hit my hot skin. I treaded water and looked all around, feeling the immense depth beneath me and that I could close my eyes and be dragged down forever. I asked the lake to remember for me and felt waves of heat emanating from my body. I gave thanks and made my way back to the ladder, looking first up the rungs, then under the pier. It would be so easy to stay under the pier, so safe and away, with the water and the memories. Then, I gazed up and willed myself to climb and emerge, to begin the journey back to NYC.

I had heard the conversations about readjustment from retreats, and I get it now. This is such a different beast than my Intro to Zen Training weekend. Time passed in Guatemala. A true week. Magic doesn't even seem like the correct word, perhaps realization is better. I've never

13

felt so in tune with nature, never witnessed nature so in tune with itself. There was harmony there, and I felt possibility for my future, for opening my heart to love not only myself, but a new man.

I changed my seat this morning so I would have a window and have been placed in an energy of a coughing child and another girl and mother moving around. I tried to sleep, but anxiety is ruling my stomach.

I don't want to go back.

I'm not going home.

I'm going to a small apartment that I'm still not comfortable in. It's not mine. My things are there, but I felt more at home in Guatemala than Astoria. There was so much space in that room. I was a world away from this life I've been forced into, from Jon, from our things. I can now understand why my yoga teacher, who is also divorced, is traveling so much. The space. I fear the confinement of Astoria. The confinement of my past, the anger, the hurt and pain of these last 8 months. Do they lie in wait for me? Can I make this space fresh, open, and a haven for me? Can I create space where there is physically so little? Can I stay true to Thomas's teachings and always remember what the 13 of us experienced, what I let go of in savasana, on the floor of my room, throwing into the fire, throwing the flower into the Lake… I cleaned my elephants; now it's time to take them for a walk down city streets.

May I be free.

May I be happy.

May I be free of suffering

and the causes of suffering.

Travel Journal Entry
7/28/13

I have all my paperwork from the week gathered to put into my journal, this beautiful witness to my journey, my experience in Guatemala.

I just re-read my last entry and remember the panic and fear that took over last night. Defining it brought tears to my eyes and allowed me to let it go, finally falling asleep on the plane.

We waited a long time for our luggage and I didn't get to my apartment until close to 4 a.m. When I went through customs, the officer stamped my passport and said, "Welcome home." I could have kissed him for that moment, as I needed it so badly. This is my home, New York City, and when I walked into my apartment, I didn't feel fear or panic. I actually looked around the bedroom and fully appreciated the work that went into making this my space, all my parents did, all I have done… it's an act of love. I meditated this morning, and tears welled and flowed as I realized there is space here. I started to feel held in this apartment for the first time, and a shift is occurring. A comfort and an acceptance of this reality and a new life. My new beginning at 38.

Remember walking into this space for the first time?

Now, a Guatemalan woman stands flowering and dancing on the kitchen wall.

Thank you, Thomas.

Thank you to my yoga teachers.

Thank you, Lake Atitlan,

    shedding off of me,

    letting go,

    whispering and letting

        it burn.

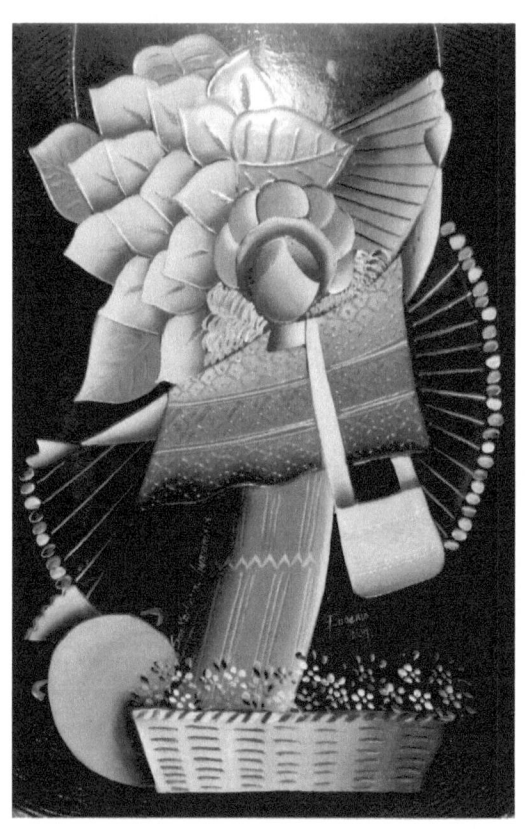

NIKÓL ROGERS

STEP 5
PASSADDHI

◆
◆
◆
◆
◆

Relaxation

SWEAT

I ROLL OVER IN THE DARK of my bedroom. The only way I know it is morning is because the clock face clicks to 7:30 a.m. on my nightstand.

A pool of sweat lays on my chest, and the sheets are wet again.

But, I don't want to lose the vision in my head, and my hand automatically reaches for my dream journal and pen.

The fan from my bathroom whirs with great force, tuning out any noise from 44th Street, and the bright light borders my closed door, giving me just enough to see my pen find a blank page.

I write down the date and feverishly start to write down my dream.

Here in my windowless bedroom.

It was all about Jon.

Again.

Every night this week.

Every night.

I watched Alfred Hitchcock's "Lifeboat" last night. I used to watch black and white movies with Jon, and loved it.

I need to get rid of pictures on my computer and don't want to face it.

I took out the trash last night and stood staring into my own window, wanting to disown this life, my reality.

Therapy Notes
8/8/13

My therapist said and I agree after re-reading my farewell poem that I have been so gracious. The relationship changed, the dynamic, and anger and picking at him were just more damaging. Self protection? Most likely.

She used the word "raw" for how things still are, and this is so true. Me coming up against my habits and conditioning of wanting speed and feeling failure if I'm not healing at a certain pace. And it's actually not about speed, but that, ultimately, I'm doing a "good job." These setbacks, these triggers and re-opening of wounds feel old, feel awful, and sometimes I just want to scream, "Can this be over?!" But it isn't, and I am trying to navigate this paradox of newfound security after Guatemala with this past, these triggers, and my old love for my marriage, all this evidence to the contrary... but as my therapist said today, "They were both true."

Isn't this life?

REHEARSAL

I'VE NEVER BEEN TO the Martha Graham studios before. In college, I soaked up every moment of my modern dance class, loving my two teachers whose foundation was Graham-based. I watched black and white films of Martha's original works from the 1950s and marveled at the dramatic lines and pure strength of her dancers.

Oh dance, I am so grateful for you.

Every week, no matter how much I was crying, I was in dance class. Every week, no matter where I was living this year, I showed up at my favorite studio to take Advanced Jazz from my best friend, Laura.

In many ways, dance was keeping me alive. Here was something from my former life that was still around, still thriving, and I would always emerge from class feeling like I could breathe better. I could reconnect with my strength as I leapt across the room and pushed from my feet into a turn.

So, when I saw an audition notice for a large dance piece, I immediately put it in my calendar.

The year had been like a wasteland for my career, after working non-stop in 2012. Everyone in the community knew what was going on, and knew Jon. We had been held up as proof that marriage could work in the theater, so it was a shock that seemed to roll like waves again and again with each person I saw. We had done a really good job of acting.

I walked into so many audition rooms to be met with sad eyes, and one choreographer actually got up from behind the table to hug me. It would have been comforting if I had been hired, but it felt like a dark cloud had been following me every time I went to audition, especially to sing. The pain was unmistakable in my voice.

I was called in for a musical revue at a theater I hadn't worked at before and prepared an upbeat song. It went great, and the director got up from behind the table to look at my song selection, asking, "Do you have a love ballad?" I froze, because I had deliberately not sung something slow for fear I would lose it, and was pretty sure I had removed all the ballads from my audition book. But there it was, *My Funny Valentine* by Richard Rogers and Lorenz Hart.

"How about this?" he smiled at me, and I felt completely stuck.

What could I say? "Oh no, sorry, I'm going through a devastating divorce and am afraid if I sing that, I will turn into a blubbering mess." Instead, I just nodded, and the pianist started the first somber notes. When I began to sing, it was as if my throat closed up. I felt possessed as I sang up to the high note, feeling like my eyes were bulging. I was forcing every last drop, and it wasn't pretty.

I finished, and the director said, "Thank you."

I couldn't get out of the room fast enough, and the casting director followed me out. It was the first time she was seeing me since the divorce. A close friend, she had actually hired both Jon and I for several jobs, plus we had spent time at her house for parties. She hugged me and said, "I am so sorry," and then rushed back into the room.

I didn't get that show either. My confidence was in the toilet, and instead of spending the summer doing theater like all my friends, I had spent it temping as an executive assistant. But quite honestly, with the robbery, I couldn't imagine being able to sing at all. I had actually been so grateful for a place to go to simply answer phones and take care of the two owners' travel arrangements.

That I could do.

And I could dance.

I felt like things were shifting, because not only did I get hired for this big dance project at Lincoln Center, but also for an outdoor revue called Broadway Under the Stars. I was actually in rehearsal for both projects at the same time, and it felt amazing to be here.

While I knew most of the dancers for Broadway Under the Stars, I barely knew any of the 100 dancers who were gathered for this other piece, and stayed more quiet than social.

This piece had been created for the 10th anniversary of 9/11, and this was its third year. And it was a mammoth piece, using sacred geometry, and performed entirely outdoors around the fountain at Lincoln Center with flowing vocals, a drum, and other instruments.

I was in NYC when 9/11 happened. I actually saw the second plane hit as I was on the elevated N train in Astoria. I was heading out to the courthouse in Queens for jury duty, and when I arrived there, all eyes were on the TV screens. It was a nightmare of a day. Somehow I made it back home after many buses, and Jon and I sat in front of the TV and just wept trying to make sense of what we were seeing.

9/11 was a real turning point for me as a New Yorker. I had been living in the city for three years and had a real love-hate relationship with the town. I loved it when I was working and auditions were going well, but hated it when I didn't have a show lined up and was having to constantly hustle. But seeing how the city pulled together in the aftermath was transformative to me.

The Martha Graham studios are so alive. I feel the history here, of so many dancers before me who danced their stories, who danced their pain.

So, I'm here, doing what I can.

I'm still dancing.

I'm still dancing.

Except now I want to dance for peace.

I line up with the other dancers, my feet and body taking me across the floor as the single drum reverberates through my being.

Dream Journal Entry
8/24/13

I go into this restaurant where I know Jon loves to have Sunday brunch and see him walk by me. I can't tell if he saw me or not. I see his bag and coat at the bar where I know he has ordered the French toast sticks.

I go into the bathroom to kill some time so as to avoid him, and there's a long line and a tourist group. There's a woman in an odd squat wheelchair waiting for a handicap bathroom, and while one handicap bathroom is open, it's too high for her. The bathroom is huge and seems to open up as I'm in there.

Then, I find myself going through a door into a huge store. My hair is a mess, in three ratty buns on top of my head. I'm walking through the Christmas decorations section. I come out of that to the cameras and electronics and realize Jon could be here, so I leave that area. I'm worried he will see me looking like this.

I have a second dream with a large bathroom.

In both of these dreams I never use the bathroom. Is this an attempted purge, but not able to follow through?

IT'S A SUNNY SEPTEMBER DAY. I grab my purse and head for the drugstore, smiling. I love how almost everything I need is so close to my apartment. I used to have to take the subway into Manhattan for most things, but now in Astoria, I can actually stay in my neighborhood. Post office, movie theater, great restaurants, and even a 24-hour organic food market. And I'm only blocks from the subway.

I love this neighborhood. It's the most convenient I have ever experienced after living in the city for 15 years.

Just five minutes from my door, I turn the corner to open the silver handle of the drugstore, and my phone rings.

"Hello, Krishna!" I answer to Adesh's brother. We have a big show coming up for the Spring Line, and I've been talking with Adesh a lot to coordinate.

"Hello Nikol... it's Adesh. He's had a heart attack."

I stay on the sidewalk.

"He's in Bombay. The traffic was horrible, and it took 30 minutes for the ambulance to get to him. He stopped breathing at that time, and is now in a coma at the hospital. We are hoping he wakes up soon."

Sun is hitting the grey cement in front of me, and people are walking by me.

"His family is flying out there. I wanted you to know first. You are going to have to do the show by yourself."

Adesh is in a coma.

"Nikol? Are you ok?"

PLANE

"REPEAT AFTER ME, I am a miracle."

I am a miracle, I say to myself.

"Hand over your heart, I am a miracle!"

"I AM A MIRACLE!" I shout out loud.

We stand in rows of ten, twelve deep, dressed in white, and all eyes and ears on the woman up front, our director and guru. She is preparing us for the performance. By her side are musicians, two flutists, three sopranos, two drummers, and a photographer.

I walked onto the grounds of Lincoln Center hours ago, while it was still dark, already dressed in white. Joining the other dancers, we gathered and ceremoniously all placed white powder on our faces to symbolize the ash that blew throughout the city on that day.

Lining up, we head outside. It's time, literally. The performance will begin at the exact moment the first plane hit Tower #1. Many people have gathered along the perimeter of the fountain. It's September 11th.

The drums begin, and we start to enter the plaza, creating three concentric circles.

We beat our sternums, singing out, and let the vibration ring through the morning air of Manhattan. We clap our hands in front of our mouths, only fingers touching, and then bring our hands out, palms offering the sound, forearms perpendicular with our bodies. Our bare feet stand firmly on the cement where we add our intention to share our message through dance with the generations who have come before to create healing through dance.

We offer our expression, we offer our silence.

I offer my expression. I offer my silence. I am so grateful to be a part of this today.

After removing white plates from each other's mantels, we all sit in the sunshine, crossed-legged, in silence, eyes lowered, listening to the flutes echoing across the plaza. We sit in three concentric circles around the main fountain, a sacred geometry.

The whole year to this point hits me so deeply in the silence. My marriage ended, the robbery, and Adesh is still in a coma. Tears drop like rain, catching the powder on my cheeks, and landing on the white plate in my lap. At the sound of the bell, I raise my plate heavenward, offering in silence pure peace to myself, to those who lost their lives, and to all who are in pain today. A plane flies overhead, and I see blue sky.

I can raise my plate of peace.

I can raise my plate of silence.

I can make an offering to heal.

I am not broken, though my heart is in deep pain.

I had worried my bare feet would bleed and tear dancing outside, but the granite is smooth and cool beneath my feet. My soles have become calloused and strengthened over the three weeks of practice, and they now carry me out of the plaza, in a line, following this community in white, all of us holding our plates at our heart centers, as the drums beat on and on.

A smile emerges after the tears.

I feel so nourished and lovingly return the white plate, until the next time of offering.

I have a feeling there will be a next time. At least now, I know I can sit at the table.

Dream Journal Entry
9/14/13

Earliest images of the night were defecating, a lot. This is the first dream of actual excrement. No bathroom, just the actual release.

I'm walking on a circular stage with my mother. We are singing along with the production. It's Les Miserables, and Dan is in the show. The stage is a giant turntable, just like in the Christmas musical. We are audience members, walking arm in arm. Mom is concerned as we pass Dan, but I tell her it's ok and encourage her to sing along. Dan never sees us.

Earlier, I'm watching a new production of Evita, a complete re-imagining. It's beautiful, there is water on the stage, completely different.

Reality Check: Adesh died yesterday. I told Laura I feel like a bowl that fills up and then keeps getting knocked over or broken. I talked about burning down again and again, and I got an email from Stacy reminding me I'm a Phoenix. I loved this reminder, and also Laura's idea to turn the loss of Adesh to gratitude that he was in my life.

BOOTH

"WHERE'S ADESH?"

This is probably the 20th time I've been asked this. The showroom gave me some extra help, and while they know Adesh has passed, the family asked us not to tell any of the retailers or customers.

So, I stand in the booth, speaking to stores that I've known for years, that I know love Adesh as much as I do, and offer, "Oh, he's in Bombay. Not able to make this show. I'll let him know you asked for him."

I then go to the corner of the booth and bawl.

I can only go to the bathroom so many times here because I have to stay in the booth.

And as I look around, I see the largest collection Adesh has ever made. I've never seen so many samples: silks, cottons, swirling patterns and vibrant colors.

He was trying so hard. So hard…

And the cavernous space of the Convention Center where Adesh and I have worked so many shows together opens up above me, the exposed ceiling of vents and wires and hanging lights.

It's been days since Krishna's phone call. His family is there with him.

And the last conversation I had with Adesh, he sounded so stressed. He wanted this collection to be the best yet. He needed it to be the best yet, as the line was struggling with making a profit.

As the lunch cart wheels by the booth, I remember Adesh happily eating green curry and drinking his Diet Coke. Smiling ear to ear, saying, "Oh, that was really spicy! So good!"

I close my eyes for a moment in the cacophony of buyers and loud conversations, and hear Adesh say, "Nikol, you are going to be ok."

No Adesh, I'm not ok. Please come back.

SILK

THEY DECIDED TO PULL THE PLUG. Adesh was actually brain dead. In those crucial 30 minutes when he had his heart attack, he lost oxygen to his brain, and never recovered. All because of the traffic.

The family had a private memoriam, and while I sent an email of condolence and flowers to his wife and family, my only contact was his brother and brother-in-law.

Adesh had been a light in my life for several years, and I had honestly wanted to grow with his company. I loved his line, and he always worked around my audition schedule. I started to see myself actually creating a career in fashion, and thought it would work well with having a family.

Not to be.

Adesh actually was the company. While his brother and brother-in-law helped with shipping and production, he was the glue, the driving force. With his tragic passing, the future of the company and his beautiful designs were completely up in the air. The family was in so much shock.

I am in shock.

And I'm speechless that I haven't heard from Jon. The three of us sat around an abundant table filled with delicious Indian dishes last year. Jon knew what Adesh meant to me, how much I believed in his clothing line, and I knew our mutual friends were talking to Jon with updates on my life. Was the divorce so deep it meant my ex wouldn't even acknowledge this loss?

Did divorce mean all communication ceases no matter what? I had gone through the process of blocking my ex on social media, and there hadn't been any emails or conversation since the apartment sold. But even when I was robbed, there was no word of concern from Jon.

I felt so alone. Jon was my harbor; he was the one I fell apart and cried in front of. This was the first death since our divorce, and I felt so disoriented not having his arms to wrap around me.

Adesh's death was a wake-up call for where the state of our relationship was. Absolute silence. And while I knew the quiet on my end was crucial for recovery, I never considered what Jon needed.

I just thought our 19 years together would count for something. Basic acknowledgement. Apparently not. We seemed to be beyond repair.

After a tortuous three days at the convention center, I had my own funeral in my apartment.

Adesh was the kindest man I had ever worked for. I never had a boss like him. He was so generous and thoughtful, teaching me all that I needed to help the line, and also constantly encouraging me in my career. He was one of my biggest cheerleaders. A true friend, and a father figure to me. During the struggle of this year, he was always there with a kind word.

Opening my closet, I look at all the beautiful samples he had sold to me and also given as gifts. I take in his designs, the vibrant swirls and crisp fabrics.

My hand gently caresses the silk sleeve of his most popular dress, the Nicole.

Different spelling, but I always felt so honored to wear it.

Goodbye Adesh. Your light went out too soon. I miss you. I miss you so much.

Dream Journal Entry
9/18/13

Am dreaming, but can barely remember; however, Dan was in my dreams the last two nights.

Last night, I dreamt I saw Dan and the feelings were back. We were in the same room together, and he was wanting to go back to how we were, and I was fighting myself.

Why now, with Adesh's passing, is Dan returning to my subconscious? He has barely been in my dreams, except for recently.

Dream Journal Entry
9/23/13

I dreamt Dan tried to make us a thing again, and I declined. I was in a show environment. He said I was different.

There were offerings of memorium to Adesh at the end of my dream, fashion pieces in his memory.

This is the first time his death has been in my subconscious.

Dream Journal Entry
9/25/13

I'm in a field with a friend for this big event. Everyone has been gathered for a kind of experiment, and I know what it is. These small pods are placed in the center, and everyone is encouraged to get close. I tell my friend the pods are full of ants, and we are meant to interact with them.

The pods explode, and it's a sea of ants moving like waves across the field. Everyone freaks out, but I stay calm and watch. The crowd has all moved behind me, and I watch the ants move and disperse. They seem to come to my feet, but no further, they are all moving out before me. My friend freaked out too. I seem to be alone in my observance and calm.

SOCKS

I'M PINCHING MYSELF RIGHT NOW. As I stand in relevé with my arms out for balance, I wait while the photographer takes shot after shot.

And he's taking them of my feet.

As a dancer, I've never been happy with my feet. I stared at professional ballerinas for years, their long lines and gorgeous arches and always wanted what they had. I wanted my foot to gracefully curve like theirs. As a teenager, I used to spend so much time stretching my feet, convincing myself that if I did that long enough, my bones would change, my feet would change. I hated the way my feet looked in pointe shoes.

I got on pointe when I was 13 and was over the moon. My mother bought me a ballet barre to practice with in my room, and I had her take a picture of me the day I got them. My hair in full 80s perm, with prep-rolled pants, and pink eyeshadow, I have the biggest grin on my face. Look at me!

Then, when I was 14, we moved to Montgomery Alabama, and I went to an Arts and Academics Magnet School, where I was going to be taking two hours of dance a day. I was placed in the advanced dance class, but when I showed up for the first day of class, all my excitement drained. I was actually one of the worst students in the class. The 12 year olds were already doing fouette turns and pirouettes in the middle of the floor, and I was still at the barre. But instead of this destroying me, it was actually the real beginning of my dance training because of the teacher.

Mrs. Carmony.

At the end of the school year, I won the award for Most Improved, and Mrs. Carmony gave me a solo. I went up to her and asked her the question that had been alive since that first day of class, "Why did you put me in the advanced level? I was so much lower than all the other girls in the class!"

Looking intently at me, she took me in and replied simply, "I saw potential in you."

Looking back at the audition video I made to get into the school, I sat in awe of what she saw. I saw an awkward 13 year old who thought she was hot stuff on pointe, but actually lacked the real strength and technique to sustain being on pointe. Mrs. Carmony, being the amazing teacher she was, saw what I could become. Thank goodness for her. She helped me discover a confidence that was healthy.

When I was 15, my family then moved to Northern Virginia, as my father was stationed at the Pentagon, and I joined a local school of ballet. I was flying high from Mrs. Carmony, from my newfound strength and confidence and was so excited to continue my growth in ballet and dance. I knew I wasn't going to be a professional ballerina, but I knew dance was going to be a part of my career, so I wanted to continue to train. Except the owners of the new school only saw my flaws. They held me back. They wouldn't let me perform on pointe my first year and criticized me constantly. I still remember the owner's long fingernail she would stick into my ribs, breathing into my ear, "Pull UP!" When they put up the cast list for The Nutcracker, my heart broke when I saw my other friends doing Snow on pointe, and I was with the younger kids in Waltz of the Flowers in flat ballet slippers.

This was when I really began to hate my feet, and while I continued to train at that studio for three years, I really doubted myself in dance and was finding an equal love in acting and singing. So, I combined the three.

Deciding to go into Musical Theater meant I didn't need to continue pointe training in college, so I retired my pointe shoes, wore flat ballet shoes, and started dancing in heels. I grew a lot in college because I had a mentor, another woman who lifted me and saw my potential. I didn't care so much about my feet, because I was finding my strength as a dancer again.

Then I became a Rockette at the age of 24 and started to see that same envy creep up as I watched many women in my line pose for pictures with striking bevels and arches that had that same beauty and grace I felt I could never achieve. Becoming a Rockette blew me away because I never pictured myself that way, but it was because of a professor from college that that job appeared. When I went to re-audition the following year to join the line again, I was told I "danced in an affected way" and was cut. The director who had sung my praises the year before now knocked me down. I was so confused.

Why did some teachers see potential and others my flaws? Was I a good dancer or not? Did I really look that terrible? I was working consistently as a performer, but it really stung when I got such cruel feedback, and I would just feel it was all my fault. It had to be the way I looked.

As a performer, I was always looking for side hustles, and would see ads for print modeling, yet would never apply. I didn't have the feet they were looking for. I didn't have that grace, and even though I was skinny, I never felt like I was skinny enough to be a model either.

When Jon dropped the bomb he was in love with a woman who was 25, every insecurity came rising, thundering from my being. I thought he saw me as beautiful. I thought he saw me for who I am, and now was facing the truth he didn't want to see me ever again.

And a rage exploded. A rage towards all of the messaging that had said I wasn't skinny enough, pretty enough, all the messages from those teachers, the directors, the choreographers, who only saw my flaws. And the rage rose as I saw the largest damage of all, how I saw myself. How all I saw was my flaws, for years. For years. I believed them. I believed Jon.

That final moment in couple's therapy was like a lightning bolt in my body. I was being torn apart, but I was also making a decision there and then that I was enough. Jon had been my compass. In giving over all my power to how he saw me, I lost complete sight of how I saw myself. I had lost any grounding around my self worth. I could see how much I had steered completely off course, and now was crashing into the rocks, breaking upon the jagged edges.

That moment in therapy woke me up. I needed to create a way of seeing myself that wasn't so critical, that wasn't based on what others thought of me. I had no idea how to do it, because that was not what I was taught, but I was going to figure it out, and I was going to ask for all the help I needed, because as the lightning tore me apart, a very young part of me was birthed. And she was innocent, young and bright pink from the canal. I promised her I would care for her, nurture her and bring her home.

So when I found Zen, and they told me I had Buddha nature, that I was whole and complete as I am, I knew I was away from the rocks. I was building my boat, piece by piece. I had a lot to learn, but for the first time in my adult life, I was embracing my self-worth.

A month after I got back from Guatemala, I ran into a dear friend on the elevator at the Equity building in NYC, where I was going for an audition. He hadn't seen me in months and knew what was going on. His face lit up when he entered the elevator and he said, "You are looking much better!"

And I smiled because I was feeling better. I had bought colorful clothes, and was settling into my neighborhood. It wasn't because my friend said I looked better that I felt better. It was simply that I *was* feeling better, and he remarked on it.

And then, a few weeks ago, I got a message from a friend on FB asking if I was looking for print modeling work. She was close friends with the owner of a sock company who was looking for a dancer to be their model. My friend had seen photos of me recently dancing and was thinking of me. She also knew I was looking for work.

She saw me. Like Mrs. Carmony, like my friend in the elevator, like my mentor in college.

So, now I am here, in a studio, wearing the coolest socks, posing.

The photographer shows me one of the photos, and as I look down at the image, all that arises in my being is, "Wow, my feet look gorgeous!"

BUTTERFLY

I'M WALKING AROUND a grassy field, in the cool morning air of October, wearing my hiking boots for the first time since Guatemala.

"Field sparrow," the guide points. In a flash, binoculars and long camera lenses all rise to capture and take in the bird happily standing on top of a long grass stalk. This is the second birding festival I've ever been to; the first was earlier this Spring.

At the age of six, I was working on a Girl Scout badge and created a binder to record what birds I saw in our small backyard on base housing in Ft. Leavenworth, Kansas. I would sit on the generator with my parents' big black binoculars and mark down all I encountered, tallying them up. My love for birds began young. Those first robins I saw on base created an awareness every time I saw something fly.

My parents' bird watching stayed very casual for most of my life, until they moved to Southern Virginia in 1994, living directly in the migratory path and within driving distance of the Eastern Shore. I listened to them go several times a year to festivals, and while I loved going on camping vacations with them, I didn't feel too much draw to really learn much more. I knew a few birds and enjoyed what I saw, but was content to just borrow their binoculars when we were together. My attention was on my career. I didn't have time for birds.

Then, on Christmas morning of 2012, I opened my big gift from my parents. I was in Astoria with Jon, praying every moment for a miracle that he would change his mind and stay. As I tore back the paper, I saw the lettering on the box, Nikon. Pulling my gift from the plastic and cardboard, I held

13

in my hands my first pair of binoculars. My own invitation to see.

Two months later, when the divorce mediation was underway, my parents invited me to fly home in April to go camping and attend a birding festival with them on the Eastern Shore. It was so healing. Not only having time with them, but I found a new spark emerging, an actual desire to learn about birds, to learn their names, their songs. It was like the six year old was alive again. She had become so silent in the face of my career and all the other things I felt were more important to learn.

And I knew this was alongside the promise I had made to myself to keep the lights on moving forward in my life. I wanted to see. I wanted to learn, and I wanted to grow. I found the bird watching to be incredibly calming. Birding seemed to go hand-in-hand with my newfound Zen practice. It was constantly inviting me into being present. One moment, the bird was there, and the next, it was gone. Sometimes you would hear a bird, but not be able to see it.

It was a constant lesson in non-attachment and impermanence.

And sometimes the bird would just sit there, giving you the opportunity to take in all its glorious colors, the gleam of its eye, and the length of its legs. I found my breath would slow and my focus sharpen. All that had occurred this year, all my pain, would fall away as I walked with the group to find a migrating warbler.

And while I was there with my parents, the binoculars around my neck now belonged to me. This was my opportunity to discover the practice of bird watching for myself.

Turns out, I love it.

Monarch butterflies are flying all around the group, and someone encourages me to put my hand out. One lands on my hand, and I have them take a picture. Oh! This is a first.

I feel all the joy of my younger self explode as I take in the simple miracle slowly opening and closing its wings, while the morning sun reflects off the vibrant spots.

"You used to be a caterpillar," I softly speak to the butterfly. "Wonder what I am becoming?"

And the butterfly takes flight, leaving me with a smile as wide as the sky.

EMAIL

I'M STARING AT THE EMAIL from Larry, asking me to coordinate and reach out to everyone I know who has worked with Sharon over the years to participate in a special event in November. This is going to be a tribute to her many years within the Stage Director and Choreography Union, as president and many other things. Larry has been her assistant for years, and was in the Christmas musical cast last year with me.

I've known Sharon for over 12 years, doing my first tour with her as a Shark girl and understudying Rosalia in *West Side Story*. In fact, I've known Larry that long as well, as he assisted Sharon for that tour.

Then, in 2008, Sharon cast me as the dance captain for the Christmas musical. That may have been the most fun I've had in a cast, except I also met Dan and started drinking very heavily. My affair began with that show, right at the end, days before closing night.

In 2010, Sharon really took me under her wing, as I shared my deep desire to start choreographing professionally, and it was her guidance and encouragement that led me to being chosen as the SDC Observer for *The Scottsboro Boys* Off Broadway at the Vineyard Theater. *The Scottsboro Boys* was hands down the most fulfilling experience I ever had in the theater. It was the first time I really experienced an artistic team that was free of ego. I was learning so much and was inspired every day by the phenomenal cast. We became a family.

When Sharon asked me to come do the Christmas musical again last year, I was very excited, but also feeling some trepidation. I had unleashed a very wild part of myself back in 2008 and began a destructive journey. Would it continue, or could I keep things together?

On the first day of rehearsal, I scanned the room and didn't feel a tug with any of the men. I felt some relief that this would be different but was also panicking because Jon was being so weird. I had just left him in New York, and he felt so distant. And I still wasn't pregnant. But, I set my sights on Thanksgiving and seeing him again. I would make that visit perfect, and we could try again.

Of course, I never expected to be confronted with my husband's affair and the fact he wanted to leave the marriage. While the first experience of the Christmas musical was ripe with late nights, drinking, and letting loose, the second experience was filled with sleepless nights, crying into my pillow, and wondering every day how I was going to show up to the dressing room and not just blurt out, "My husband wants to end our marriage."

The Christmas musical was also the last full musical I had done out of town. This year brought some opportunities for local gigs, but my auditions were bringing the same result: silence.

Sharon was someone very important in my life. She had always been a cheerleader and guide in my career. I was honored to be a part of organizing her tribute. So, I knew I would do whatever Larry was asking, and yet. . .

While Sharon and Larry knew about my divorce, neither of them knew about the affair. In fact, very few people did. This was where I felt the deepest shame. I was still hiding it from most people.

At the end of 2012, I was so desperate for couple's therapy to work, and wanting to believe that 2013 was going to heal my marriage, I called Dan on New Year's Eve and left a voicemail telling him to never call or text me again. My biggest priority was saving my marriage. It was over. And I meant it this time, not like all the other times I had said it was over. This had to be the end.

And now, as I look at this email from Larry, I know what this means.

It means it's time to email Dan. This will be my first contact since that voicemail on New Year's Eve. And it doesn't matter if this is a group email.

I compose all the information about the tribute. And I hit send.

Was this what you wanted, Adesh?

Is this why Dan has been so active in my dreams since you passed?

Is this what I actually want?

CONTACT

I'M READING THE EMAIL.

It's more than I could have ever hoped for, and I feel surprised, encouraged, and open. This is a side of Dan I always looked for but rarely experienced, as we were usually drunk together, and the relationship was soaked in our collective shame.

He's saying he wanted to reach out but didn't think it right considering my message from New Year's Eve.

He's saying the last thing he wants to do is disrespect my wishes.

He's saying he would love to support Sharon, but the most important thing is respecting what I need right now.

He's saying if I want to talk, he will be there.

He's saying he wishes me the absolute best.

And something shifts inside. I'm not scared, and I want to bring closure to this relationship. I'm ready to see him, in a very different way.

Adesh, I'm listening. I'm ready.

Email to Dan

10/31/13

In truth, I have been asking to see you, hoping actually, because I am feeling like I am ready to see you, in person, and truly have a real conversation about what has happened this year, and about me. When Larry contacted me a week ago, I was put in charge of contacting cast members. I knew this would mean emailing you, and I welcomed it, and its timing.

To say this year has been a journey is such a deep truth. I never knew if you were angry at me for that phone call on New Year's Eve. The year has been the biggest lesson in impermanence and change, and I have burned to ash in the loss and abandonment. Thankfully, I have been supported by my "net" and wanted more than anything to survive the deep despair, so I did, and I continue to heal.

I would very much like to see you, to have a talk face to face, free of the karma of our past, free of alcohol. I was so touched by your email, and your genuine concern. I struggled very much with reaching out to wish you a Happy Birthday, but didn't want to upset you if you truly wanted a clean break as well. I'm heartened to hear of your new relationship, and my wishes are still the same, for your happiness.

Let's find a time to sit. Thankfully, now, I am far more aware of my actions.

See you soon,

Niki

STEP 6
SAMADHI

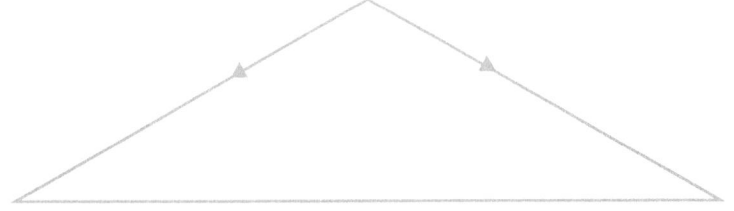

Mental Equilibrium

DINNER

I'M EATING, AND LISTENING, but something is very different.

I don't feel the pull. I don't feel the twinge in my gut, the draw on my body, feeling like I am out of control and have no choice but to indulge.

I sit across from Dan and actually feel grounded. I'm not pleading with him to tell me why I keep returning to our affair. I'm not feeling like I want to jump across the table and kiss him, or secretly am playing out what we will do later.

I'm actually just listening to him.

And he feels completely different to me. He's no longer the refuge for my unhappiness. He's actually a friend. Or maybe something even more neutral.

I've shared about my year, how hard it's been, my journey, and he's more present than I have ever experienced. Usually, we were both drunk with each other, so conversation didn't get too deep. But now, I feel heard and actually supported, which is what I was chasing after in all the wrong ways before in our relationship.

I never wanted to leave my marriage for Dan. But I was now learning in therapy that I had wanted to leave, I was just terrified to admit this to myself. Dan wasn't the next love of my life, he was actually how I was hiding from myself; he was my self destruction because I didn't want to listen to or face what was really going on. I had said it was over to him so many times, and we wouldn't see each other for up to a year, but then something would happen, and I would go right back to him. Back to the bottle, back to killing the pain. And every time I did go back, I felt even more ashamed, and scared. So many times, I was screaming to myself, "Why am

I doing this? Why do I keep doing this? I always feel like shit after! Why can't I stop?"

He was my addiction.

And now, sitting across from him, I feel sober. I am sober.

After four years of pounding my fists against the wall after we would see each other, and crying in the shower so my husband didn't hear, the pull was gone.

What a miracle.

If this is possible, what else can heal?

I take another bite and enjoy the food in my mouth, the taste and texture. Sipping through my straw, the cool iced tea drips down my throat, cooling my insides, as I listen to Dan.

The fire is burning within, but it's being fueled by something very different now. I don't want to punish myself anymore.

The answer was never in Dan. It was always in me.

CRACK

THEIR LAUGHTER IS SO CONTAGIOUS. I can't stop smiling. The sun reflects off their blond hair as they climb the slide again and again. Surrounded by the changing leaves of early November, I can't help myself and start taking as many pictures as possible.

I was the first to hold them in the hospital almost two years ago, so tiny and miraculous. Jon and I each held one, and I could feel my whole body alive with desire. Laura was laying in the bed, post C-section, and smiling at us. I felt so honored to be meeting them on their second day of life.

Just the year before, we had gone to a Paul McCartney concert, and Laura said she had something to share with us and pulled out an ultrasound of not one heartbeat, but two. Her eyes were so bright! Seeing her journey gave me the courage to finally get off the pill myself, and I did on my next birthday in 2011.

Laura knew how much I wanted to be a mother, and when my marriage imploded, I spent many weekends up at her house, changing diapers, reading stories to the twins, and soaking up their growing joy.

And now they have a slide, swings, and a playset in their yard. And so we play, all together.

I follow Jessie and James around to the front of the house, just taking in their curiosity as they touch the grass and explore every inch of the yard. Jessie touches the bark of a tree and looks back at me with her big blue eyes, so open and calm.

I take a picture of her and then accidentally drop my phone.

When I pick it up, I see a crack across the screen.

Oh no...

What do they say? Is this bad luck?

Maybe it's nothing. I've already been through so much already. I'll just get it fixed tomorrow.

SHOULDER

I'M DRIVING BACK FROM Laura's after sharing the pictures with her and hugging the twins. It was such a wonderful Sunday afternoon.

I'm on the expressway, and traffic is usual, fast and full, but I've been driving in the city for 11 months now, and feel pretty comfortable. I've made the drive to and from Laura's many times.

Suddenly, a car cuts in front of me and slams on its brakes, and before I know it, I've rear-ended them.

I stop breathing for a moment, and it's like everything is whizzing past me. We both slow down and hug the left lane as much as possible, because there is no shoulder on this expressway. I put on my flashers and pray no one else is going to hit my car.

It seems pretty straightforward to me, but the other driver is insistent it's my fault, and we are both on the phone with our insurance. The damage is minimal to their car, and minimal to mine.

Cars are starting to slow, and we have created a complete traffic jam. Everyone is staring at us.

I report the accident and get the other driver's information, and my insurance asks, "How far away from home are you?"

"Only about 15 minutes," I say.

"Ok, once you are home, give us a call back, and we will go over everything and create the full report."

Once I have the agreement with the other driver, we both slowly edge back out of traffic, and I start to practice deep breathing.

I'm ok. I'm ok. I'm ok.

But the cracked screen was the first, and the car accident was the second. What will be the third?

Will there be a third?

WATER BOTTLE

I'M ALMOST HOME, LITERALLY blocks from my apartment. I feel like I'm breathing again and enter into an intersection with a green light. There is a big white van parked on the street, so I can barely see any clearance. I edge into the intersection with caution.

There is an explosion of sound in my ears.

Hit squarely on the passenger side, my body jerks to the left and then the right violently. I'm spun in a circle and find myself on the opposite sidewalk, still inside my car.

A huge, dark Jeep is in front of me. The airbag hasn't gone off.

Oh my GOD… I've been hit.

I've just been in a second car accident.

I've just been in two car accidents in a row…

My mind starts to race, and my heart is pounding in my ears as my body starts shaking.

And the first thing I think as I'm clutching to the steering wheel is, "Is *this* enough, Jon? Is this enough for you to speak to me? Will you speak to me now?" The sting of his silence in the face of Adesh's passing now burning hot. He knew better than anyone what Adesh meant to me, and I was stunned to hear nothing. We spent 19 years of our lives together. How do you just stop speaking to someone you loved? Have I become completely invisible to him? Has he lost every ounce of humanity or care towards me?

Is a car accident enough?

I then look outside and internally ask, "Am I going to die today? If I get out of this car, what else is going to happen?"

A man knocks on my window and asks me if I am ok. I open my door, and he hands me a small water bottle, telling me he's a cop off duty and saw the whole thing. It appears he is the owner of the white van that was blocking the intersection.

I somehow emerge from my car and take in the water bottle, hearing a voice in my head saying, "When you are in shock, be sure to stay hydrated."

I come around to the passenger side of my car and stop breathing. It's totaled. The silver metal caved in across the passenger front and back sides. The owner of the Jeep that hit me is now screaming at me, "Did you not SEE me?" Are you BLIND?!"

Shock is setting in on so many levels. I can't believe this driver thinks this is my fault. I can't believe my grand-mother's car, the first car I have ever owned, is completely totaled.

I can't believe I've been in two car accidents in one day. I've been in two car accidents within an hour.

I was almost home.

And I'm all by myself. Am I going to die today?

My shoulder starts to hurt, and my right leg. I look down and see a big bruise forming on my right arm.

And just then, the tow truck pulls up. Everything feels like it's happening at warp speed.

I have never been in an accident like this before, and I'm all by myself and in shock.

Oh grandma, I am so sorry. I am so sorry.

SIGNATURE

I'M SITTING IN THE passenger side of the tow truck, and he's handing me a paper to sign. "What is this for?" I ask.

"Oh, it's all routine," he responds and then starts to explain parts of the contract, though I can't seem to make sense of anything he is saying. He's assuring me he's taking my car to a safe place. He's assuring me this is the only option I have. He's assuring me I will be able to get my car back. I literally have no idea what to do right now.

He's assuring me, so I sign the contract and shakily exit the truck.

I then walk directly to a walk-in clinic, getting there just minutes before they close, as it's a Sunday and they have shorter hours. The doctor looks me over and states my injuries are not severe. The bruise is starting to throb, and now that I've done some walking, I know nothing is broken.

Except my confidence.

Except any ray of hope that things were getting better.

I slowly walk back to my apartment and call my insurance for the second time today, not just to fully report and go over the first accident on the expressway, but the second that happened just blocks from my home.

There is a silence on the other side of the line when I tell them I've just been in another accident. And another silence when I tell them about the tow truck. I really had no idea what I was doing.

After I hang up, I call my mother and weep. I call Laura, and she can't believe this happened. I can't believe it. I can't believe this is my life.

When is this year going to end?

I'm alive today, and I'm walking, but it's only the beginning of November.

I do finally fall asleep, but no dreams come. Just darkness and breath. Darkness and breath.

RENTAL

"I'M GOING TO TEAR your car apart, piece by piece," he says slowly and menacingly into my ear. I'm holding my phone, but my hand is going numb.

Apparently, the document I signed from the assuring tow truck driver signed away my rights to the car, and since it has been deemed undrivable, the owner of the lot is telling me he owns my car now and is going to sell it off for scraps.

I have ZERO idea if he is even telling the truth.

I hang up the line and immediately call my insurance again, and relay the threat to which they say, "We are sending over an investigator right away."

When my phone does ring again, I'm speaking directly to the investigator, who shares with me how amiable the lot owner was and directed him to my car right away when he showed his badge. Of course, speaking completely differently to the male investigator than he did over the phone with me, a woman.

Now my insurance has the car.

It's out of the lot.

And it's totaled.

My insurance is going to give me the full blue book value for the car, and I realize this is why the lot owner wanted it so badly. He knew it still had value. Maybe I'll buy another car… or maybe I'll just put it in savings right now. I don't really have any savings right now.

And then I remember, I'm supposed to drive to my alma mater in five days to see my mentor's one-woman show.

I'm going to have to get a rental. And I'm going to have to drive again.

I'm going to have to drive again…

NEEDLE

BECKY HAS TRULY BEEN my guardian angel. She texted me out of the blue last December when I first got back from Utah, asking, "How are you?"

Because she was one of my closest friends, I told her the truth. "Jon and I are in terrible trouble." She then sent over the name of a couple's therapist, who was able to see us within days, and who then became my guiding light.

And later in the year, she recommended her acupuncturist. I had never had acupuncture before, but when I met Sally for the first time, she looked at me with the biggest eyes and simply asked, "How are you?" I knew I was in the presence of a healer and started going weekly.

She listened with intent, checking my pulses, and guiding me through all the ways my body was expressing grief, anger, and shame.

My chest had exploded in red bumps in the spring, and she explained how my night sweats were my body's way of releasing all the extra heat, all the emotional pain. A long line had formed down the center of my tongue, signaling my broken heart, and turning a more ashen gray, void of the vibrant red color that existed in happier days.

So, two days after the accidents, I walk into Sally's treatment room after work to share what had happened.

"Let's start with your back," she gently offers.

I lay my face into the cradle and gently place my bruised arm beside me. As my body begins to relax, Sally places a needle in my mid back, and it sears white hot, intense and alive.

"Oh!" I exclaim. And then I start crying and can't stop.

It's flowing out of me in waves, cascading with force.

Sally gently strokes my arm, making sure I'm ok, and then leaves me in the dark room.

Somehow, the tears do stop, and the point in my back that was so painful subsides. I feel like I've experienced a deep release. I feel tender and better.

When Sally comes back in, she quietly says, "It's a good thing you came in so soon after the accidents, before the fear set into your muscles."

I had no idea that even happened. Is this how my body actually works?

"IF YOU FALL OFF A HORSE, just get back up on the saddle again."

Or maybe in my case, if you are in two car accidents in one day and think you are going to die, get back behind the wheel and drive again. And do it within 5 days. And do it by yourself.

Oh, and drive to a place that is going to definitely be a HUGE trigger for your breaking heart.

As I left the rental car lot earlier this morning, I had a moment when I couldn't find my breath. My hands were shaking as I turned the key in the ignition. But I was resolute on going. My arm was ok, and this trip was important. As the hours passed, and I found myself looking out at Pennsylvania roads, I found I was still alive. I was driving with caution, but nothing was hitting me.

I was driving again... somehow.

I felt a world of turmoil within me for where I was actually driving to. My mentor from college, Paula, was doing her one-woman show after announcing her retirement from teaching. She was the original head of the dance department for the musical theater BFA program and had been a guiding light for me.

As the road stretched in front of me, I remembered Paula handing me her dance captain book from *Merlin* on Broadway. When she did, I felt I was holding gold in my hands. Paula had just cast me as the dance captain for our college production of the musical *She Loves Me*, and I was only a sophomore. Paula held my hand, teaching me how to write down all the patterns on stage and map out where each cast member was.

This experience paved the way for six more professional shows where I would be hired as the dance captain, and each time, I felt so prepared because of the semester Paula handed me her Broadway bible. When I had come to college as a freshman, I was really the only trained dancer, and Paula made sure I was challenged and helped me to grow. She encouraged me and always saw my potential. Her teaching helped shape the professional dancer I would become, and she nurtured this skill I loved. After feeling like I was never good enough as a dancer in the school of ballet I had just spent my high school years in, Paula's classes were a great sigh of relief.

Paula had then transitioned from being my mentor to also being a friend as I moved to NYC and began my career. She began to share more about her life and her struggle in an unhappy marriage, and becoming a single mother after divorce. And she shared how she too found Buddhism when her life was falling apart.

So, regardless of the car accidents, I was going to somehow see her show, stay with her, and support this big moment.

But, this was the first time I was going to be returning to my alma mater in 13 years. I had been there for a wonderful few weeks choreographing their summer production of *Little Shop of Horrors* in 2000, but I had not been back since then.

Back to where it all began. Meeting Jon. Falling in love with Jon. Getting engaged to Jon.

13 years.

I drive into town, and my heart is burning in my chest. Everywhere I look, there are memories. I park the car near the theater to meet up with Paula after her sound check and final dress rehearsal and walk into a brand new theater built off campus. It is beautiful, and Paula is overjoyed to see me.

"I'm so glad you are here!" she exclaims. Her hug feels really good and soothing to my body.

After getting a quick tour, I tell her that I will meet her at her home soon.

I decide to go for a walk in the dark November air. So much of the campus has radically changed, but I feel drawn towards the landmarks that are still standing and look the same. The lights of the Old Main Building shine bright, and I take a picture to remember. I then walk to a favorite restaurant, seeing the hustle and bustle of diners coming in and out, just as they did when I lived here. So, I take another picture to remember.

Then, I walk down a side alley to stand in front of a nondescript building. It appears empty, the contents gone. Witnessing the faded yellow siding, I remembered coming here two days a week my final semester of college. The dance shop was a place of joy for me, and the whole reason I took the job was to pay for Jon's wedding ring. In my memory, this building was the color of a summer sun. For a moment, I hesitate. Do I want to remember this? But my hands go to my phone, and I take a picture of the deserted building. This is the first thing that actually looks like I feel.

I drive to Paula's and am greeted by purring cats and a hot meal. It is wonderful to be with her alone, and this is the first time I fully unload all that has been happening.

That night, I dream of a giant storm, thunder, lightning and crashing waves of water. That night, I cry myself to sleep.

GHOST LIGHT

IN THE SUMMER OF 2007, I performed in a production of the musical *Chess*. It was a huge win for me, being cast in a rock musical, as I was rarely considered for this genre and felt like my voice was only getting stronger. I was also working with a Broadway director and choreographer that I adored at a regional theater that was quickly becoming my second home.

I had seen the musical for the first time when I was 12 on the West End and remember being blown away by the sound and the stage, laid out like a giant chess board rising up for the audience to see.

However, as a 12 year old, the subject matter of the musical was way over my head, and I sang along to the cast album not really understanding what I was saying. But when rehearsals for the same musical began for me at the age of 32, and the subject of infidelity came up, and being unhappy in marriage, something was stirring. I had experienced major show crushes with leading men in several shows I had done but seemed to think I was exempt because nothing ever happened, and wasn't I happily married?

That production of *Chess* was highly sexual, and all my energy, all my doubts, were channeled into writhing on long metal poles and dancing as if my life depended on it. I didn't have any show crushes in that production, so the energy had to go somewhere.

The cast was very close, and I was in awe of the two leading females, both singing with enormous voices that echoed through the halls. They both had these giant ranges, and I would listen to them, feeling their vocal power go through my bones. I longed for that kind of power, and while I had some really amazing moments as a singer up to this point in my career, I really doubted myself because those moments were not consistent like they were with my dancing.

Of the two leading women, Christy was very close with her leading man. As they were both in committed relationships, I watched this with both disgust and fascination. I began to create a complete fantasy that she was having an affair, even though there was no proof this was happening. I found myself wanting to know more and at the same time judging myself for wanting to know more. There was a war happening inside me, and many times I would find myself wanting to burst through her dressing room door and just ask, "Are you having an affair?" Probably to quiet my rage and also to ask how she was actually doing it.

Christy and I stayed friends after the show closed, and really began to talk more when she decided to go back to school for her MFA in vocal pedagogy at my alma mater. When my life fell apart, she reached out with support and loving words, so with my planned trip to see my mentor's show, Christy and I had set aside the daytime to hang before Paula's show at night.

We begin at the Waffle Shop, which has moved locations to a completely different part of campus and become a large restaurant. Still as packed as its former version, we sit down in a booth and soon have piping hot waffles on colorful ceramic plates. I can't even remember how many times I ate off these same plates in the five years I went to school here, or the countless times Jon and I ate at the Waffle Shop together when he would visit.

Over home fries and scrambled eggs, I inhale and then exhale all that has happened this year.

Christy's eyes are big and taking in every word, and she takes a sip of tea and then opens up about how she's struggling in her marriage. They are working through it, and she wants to work through it, but it's really tough.

Grabbing my hand, she says, "I'm here for you today. I can only imagine how weird and hard it is being back here."

We leave the Waffle Shop and make our next stop at the Nittany Lion monument. A tradition for every student and every alumni, I have so many pictures—beginning with arriving as a freshman, to taking pictures with my brother when he was also going to school here, to posing with Jon. I have pictures of riding the lion, of hanging upside down from it, and also just standing next to it. And the monument is the same. It's in the same place, in a pose of readiness, mid-walk, looking directly at the viewer with strength.

A fellow student is kind enough to take the obligatory picture of Christy and I smiling on either side of the lion's head, and after, I ask Christy if she could take some photos of me. I'm feeling better and sit side saddle on the lion, making it look like I am riding it with ease. And then I ask Christy to take a picture of me kissing the lion, an act of gratitude. Maybe this can be a healing experience for me, being back here. Maybe I can create new memories here.

Feeling emboldened, we walk towards the theater building, the place I spent the bulk of my time. As I open the outside doors to the hallway, I feel my throat start to tighten. The hallway is exactly the same as it was 13 years ago. I walk to the end of the hallway to peek into the main rehearsal space, Studio 19. The hardwood floors and the wall of mirrors all speak to me, bringing up a wave of memories and images.

Seeing Jon in a production of *Bent* when I was a freshman and feeling so alive, overcome with desire for him and so in awe of his acting ability. Being in rehearsal for *Evita* the summer after my freshman year, and Jon sitting in a rocking chair and staring at me as I danced, and then asking on the break, "Would you like to have lunch together?" Being in rehearsal for *Children of Eden* the summer after we got married, and Jon making me laugh until tears streamed down my face for the silly bunny character he created for Noah's Ark.

I tear myself away from the swinging doors and walk down the steps to the black box theater, Studio 6, where all the late-night underground student productions were performed. "Try it this way," I hear Jon say, coaching me on the One Act play I'm in. Every direction he offered worked. The audience laughed, and I actually thought for a moment I could be funny.

And further down the hallway, down by the dressing rooms, are steps leading up. "Christy, can you please come with me?"

I climb the steps to enter backstage of the main theater, the Mainstage. And now, the images are forming all around me as I walk onto the stage.

Jon turning to tell me he loves me for the first time. Jon kneeling down to ask me to marry him. Here, it all began. Here, we fell in love. I feel like a knife is ripping into my heart, and I can't feel my feet.

I sink down onto the floor and weep, breaking wide open. Big sobs erupt from my mouth and echo through the seats, up the rafters, and along the heavy curtains. Wave after wave, and I hold my heart, just like in the bathroom and say internally, "This too."

The waves crest; they explode and then begin to ebb. Slowly, gently, my breath begins to come back in, and I look up at Christy, her big eyes of grace taking me in. She's looking at me with care, and I say, "Christy, you are my guardian angel. I can't imagine coming back here by myself. I am so grateful you are here. Thank you, thank you, thank you."

And I share with her all the memories I'm seeing, and she listens. She listens.

And I realize that even though this year has been the worst year of my life, in every one of these horrible situations of loss, I have had support. The people I have needed have come into my life. Laura on the phone on Black Friday after Jon dropped the bomb. My mother was there to help me to create a list for mediation when I couldn't see straight. The lab technician who told me I actually had strong lungs when my cough wouldn't go away. Beth offering me a place to stay when I was losing my home. Kumar calling to guide me through doing the fashion show without Adesh. The investigator returning my car to my insurance company after I was threatened they would sell it for parts, And now, Christy, sitting beside me as I sob on the floor.

I haven't made it this far alive alone. I am not alone. A close friend had said to me back in January, "You spent years creating a net, and now it's time to fall back into it." This has been the largest lesson of the year, learning how to actually accept help. I thought I was weak if I asked for help. I thought I could handle my life on my terms. I was wrong. And this year has shown me again and again the magic of interdependence. I raised my palms to the heavens last November and cried, "I need help!"

And it came. It has come. It is here with me right now.

There's a big set for the Fall production of *Guys and Dolls* on the Mainstage, and right in the middle of the stage is a ghost light. A ghost light is a single bulb that is switched on whenever the theater is dark, but many also believe the ghost light's main function is to chase away mischievous spirits, and/or create warmth and centering for the ghosts that inhabit the theater.

I smile at the light and for this encounter with my ghosts here. The light is warming and centering. I feel stronger after releasing all my pain, and Christy and I walk out to enjoy a bite to eat.

ANNIVERSARY

"PLEASE PREPARE FOR LIFT-OFF. Put your items beneath your seat and make sure your tray tables are secured."

It's Thanksgiving Day, and at 9 a.m., the plane rises into the skies above LaGuardia Airport heading to Norfolk, Virginia.

9 a.m., when I would normally be seated in front of the TV, brimming with excitement for the Macy's Thanksgiving Day parade. A tradition I enjoyed in childhood but that really became significant in my marriage. Wearing our pajamas, holding steaming mugs of hot chocolate, we would snuggle, dance along to the musical numbers, and wait with anticipation for Santa Claus. At the end of the parade at noon, Jon would officially declare it was holiday season and break out Christmas music.

A day of joy, a day of celebration.

Until last year.

Today is the anniversary of everything falling apart. Today, a year ago, I watched the Macy's parade with the cast and then sat in anticipation for my then-husband's arrival. Today, I watched the man I was married to kneel in front of me and say he doesn't love me anymore. So, when I booked my flight to go home to my parents, I knew what I wanted to avoid.

The flight has a layover in DC, and then lands in Norfolk at 12:30.

No parade this year.

Thank goodness.

As I see NYC disappear from view, I feel my whole body relax.

Dream Journal Entry
11/29/13

I'm back at Penn State, and the triggers from before are gone. I'm turning over my position to someone else and trying to coordinate the last bit of paperwork. The new person taking my position is much younger, and I say to her, "If you see a ring on someone's hand, don't bother."

* Reflections—Yesterday was Thanksgiving and ended so lovely. Was so healing to be with my parents to focus on gratitude, and I felt possibility for the Christmas season that I can make it my own with new memories, not just re-living the trauma.

STEP 7
UPEKKHA

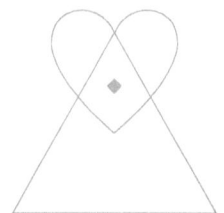

Introspection

CAMERA

LOOKING DIRECTLY INTO THE CAMERA, I exhale. The lens is very close to my face, a black orb of glass and metal stretching endlessly.

"That's a wrap!" the director yells.

I get up off the bed, and he comes over to me smiling. "That was great! You are all set. You can relax downstairs while we take care of the other shots."

I hug my teenage "son" on the bed, who also smiles at me. "Can we take a picture together?" I ask.

"Absolutely!" he nods with enthusiasm. I ask a crew member to take a picture of us, and then I give him a big hug and leave the bedroom so he can prepare for the next scene.

I go to the bathroom to change and take a moment to just look in the mirror. I'm actually amazed at how calm I am. I thought I would be nervous on actual shoot day, but I was really grounded in my body. I felt really good about the scene.

I took my first on-camera class in 2011, and it was sobering. My expressions and reactions were way too big on camera. I was so used to performing on big stages, this was something altogether new. With the lens being so close and intimate, I had to learn how to make everything small, subtle, and focused.

Last year I spent a lot of time working on my on-camera technique. Jon and I actually used to get together with another married couple in our neighborhood and practice scenes together. We hooked a camera up to our TV and then would watch each other. It was really frustrating for me. I would work on the scenes, and then when I was watching myself, I seemed to have this crazy tick in my eyes. My eyes would dart from left to right when I had to look in the camera or at my scene partner. The other couple had more on-camera experience, and I just felt like I wasn't measuring up. And Jon always seemed to just nail his scenes. I wanted to exhibit that ease they all did and wanted to step out of the box of being just a musical theater performer.

But, the camera terrified me. I was so afraid to be seen. Could the camera see the pain I was trying to hide? Would it telecast that I was lying to everyone around me? Would the camera expose that I was just putting on an act, having an affair, and mortified I wasn't pregnant?

A few months ago, as I was returning to performing again, I decided I wanted to also return to auditioning for on-camera work. I took a workshop that felt different from the others I'd taken and got some very encouraging feed-back, so I decided to go audition for a student film. I had never done that before, and I booked it. I was over the moon! I had never been in a short film before, having only done a few commercials with no speaking.

Rehearsal over the last month was an absolute joy. It felt so rewarding to be working on a character, and also with a cast that all really cared about the project. And I loved that I was cast as a mother. It felt like a confirmation of my deep-est desire.

But what I noticed the most was how calm I was in my body. I wasn't questioning myself or constantly criticizing myself as I had in the past. I really was just having fun!

And today, as the camera came in close, I didn't flinch.

I wanted to be seen.

I'm ok with being seen.

I don't have anything to hide anymore.

Most of all, I don't want to hide anymore.

FAMILY

I HAVEN'T BEEN TO MY AUNT and uncle's house since I was 5 years old. They owned and ran a design company in San Diego that kept them very busy, so international traveling to see us when we lived in Europe didn't happen.

I have happy memories of my uncle when I was very young visiting my grandparents' house in Pennsylvania. I can remember hearing his gregarious laughter ringing through the house during the holiday as my brother and I zoomed around the living room in cardboard cars. As a child, I had no idea that he was also drunk.

My interactions with my aunt and uncle were few and far between, receiving cards for birthdays and holidays, and then every few years seeing them for family gatherings, weddings, and big birthdays.

The last time I saw them was 2009, when we all gathered at the beach. I didn't see much of my uncle during that week, as he was suffering from severe back issues and painful digestion. He had been sober for decades by that point, but I really didn't know who he was.

Earlier this year, he was diagnosed with Alzheimer's, and it was starting to really progress, so my parents and I did something we had never done before. We decided to have Christmas in San Diego with them.

I was thrilled to have a completely new experience this Christmas just to create a brand new memory and erase the horror of last year, so I boarded the plane with relief and expectation.

The sunshine of California felt amazing on my skin when I touched down, and seeing my parents brought great joy. As I entered my aunt's house, I felt a small remembering in my body from being here at five years of age, but mostly it was strange and new. And then I saw my uncle.

He smiled at me but had no idea who I was. His belt was notched tight around a waist that was shrinking. He would go in and out of knowing my mother, but my father was also a stranger. And my aunt was in a constant state of management, with my mother right by her side wanting to help her sister in any way possible.

We did some local birding, and my uncle became very upset and agitated when he was told he couldn't go into the water and play with the birds. He swung from moments of quiet to anger and aggression very quickly.

And I heard him say, "Who is that girl?" as he would look at me sideways.

I returned his gaze, thinking, "Oh, uncle, I still don't know you, and perhaps you never knew me either. Distance makes relationships very hard to grow." I had immense proof with my marriage falling apart. We spent so much time away from each other.

Christmas morning was very emotional, and I was so grateful to be waking up in a different place. My mother was doing all she could to make the day special, and my aunt had Christmas music playing.

For years, I had written a holiday poem and given it to family and friends. This year I wrote something special just for my parents and aunt. I poured my heart out in the piece, and both my aunt and mother wept reading it, hugging me, and encouraging me.

And my father sat on the couch, holding the poem with a dry eye, mumbling about how writers don't make any money.

I took in my father sitting there, remembering all his comments when I was in high school about how he could use his influence with the Pentagon to get me a job in the CIA. Smiling enthusiastically, he'd talk about how I could use my acting ability and great grades to be an agent. Or the visits to NYC where he would expound on what a great path it would be to teach at a university. I found this so confusing, as he would also sit in the audience of my shows and cheer loudly. Wasn't what I was doing enough?

And I took it in for years. Even though I never wanted to be a CIA agent. I tried to laugh it off and make it a family joke, but my laughter was getting tighter. I loved teaching but also loved performing and at the time didn't want to end my career and make such a huge switch. But most of all, I think I just wanted my father's approval.

Such a young part of me was just waiting for Daddy to say, "This is good. You are good enough."

And some new thoughts arose on this Christmas Day. What if my father was anxious all along about my career path and was worried about me struggling? Indeed my career on stage had been a dramatic roller coaster of highs and lows, all of which he heard. My father had chosen a very secure and different path than I, working his whole career with the military, even though he went to college for Astronomy. And this year, he just retired. He was going through a big life change himself.

What if all those conversations that drove me crazy were his way of showing love?

And most of all, what if I accepted my father for who he is? Fighting never seemed to work. Fighting never changed his views or beliefs, and there were so many heated moments between us growing up. The loud voices banging off the walls certainly didn't make us closer in those moments, which was what I really wanted.

I really wanted connection with my father, not approval.

Maybe approval could come from another source. Maybe approval could come from within myself.

So, I let my father be on the couch, and instead, I received a hug from my mother as she said, "One day, you have to write a book."

And Thomas's face flashed before me, his pencil outlining my Mayan birth chart in the Guatemalan sun.

Maybe I will, and it will be about this year.

A Christmas gift indeed, not in the form I expected, but what I needed to move forward.

In the afternoon, I put on a Santa hat and ask my aunt to take a picture of me sitting on her diving board in one of Beth's old bathing suits she had given to me when I lost so many clothes. As I look at the camera, I feel something I haven't felt in a long time.

I feel beautiful, and I want to be seen as a woman. I want my femininity to be seen.

I want to be seen as the woman I am now.

FIRE

IT'S OFFICIALLY 2014, the first hour of the New Year, just after midnight. My parents' house seems very quiet, especially after the bustle of the airport and plane ride back to their house from San Diego earlier today. Sinking into the couch, I take in the moment of being alone downstairs, my parents now asleep upstairs. Our colorful hats and streamers sit on the living room table where we all placed them moments ago after counting down loudly to herald in 2014.

But I have one more thing to do to close out 2013. I'm not quite ready for the New Year yet.

On the plane earlier today from my aunt's house in San Diego, I read a blog post about how powerful this moment is, the end of a year and the beginning of a new one. The author offered a ritual to release what no longer serves you to make way for the new.

I was completely enmeshed in this article on the plane. I had never done something like this before. New Year's Eve had always been about parties, drinking, and loud noises with loud music. I came up with "resolutions" each year, but this was something far stronger, deeper, and now with my Zen practice, I really understood the difference.

Standing around the fire Thomas made in Guatemala woke in me something that had been asleep. It awoke in me the power of ritual.

I thought I had rituals in my life before. I used to snooze my alarm once or twice every morning, then go into the bathroom and turn on the radio for my shower, then do some stretching and put on my makeup and warm up my voice before an audition. Except as I learned, this was actually more of a routine. Yes, this routine set me up for my auditions, but it wasn't setting me up for a nourishing beginning to my day, or allowing me to connect with my well being or confidence. I began with doubt, anxiety, and noise and then just filled myself with even more noise to get through my inner critic yelling at me when the audition didn't go the way I wanted.

But ritual... very different.

Now I had a daily ritual. I would light a candle, light some incense and place the burning stick in ash, and then sit down to meditate. When my timer went off 10 minutes later, I would grab a set of mala beads that were given to me as a gift and hold them in my hand, the smoothness of rose quartz gliding along my forefinger and thumb as I said a mantra.

And since starting this ritual, my whole way of being had changed drastically. I wasn't shutting down in the face of challenges. I wasn't drinking to escape, and I wasn't playing loud music to drown out my thoughts. For the first time in my life, I was actually facing each day as it happened. These last 13 months had created a deep transformation for how I showed up in the world.

And I was starting to hear something far wiser deep within me. I never really understood what intuition was, but this voice was calm and helpful. Was it there all along?

On the plane ride earlier today, while coming back home from San Diego, I followed the author's instructions. I wrote down what I wanted to release from the year. And I really took my time with this, reflecting on the divorce, my robbery, Adesh's death, and the car accidents.

I thought of the pain, the moments of being curled in the fetal position, and hours of therapy as I wept. And I thought of the power of fire. How I had felt like who I was as a person was burning to ash again and again this year. My identity as a wife? Burned to ash. My identity as an expectant mother? Burned to ash. My identity as an adulterer? Burned to ash.

What about my identity as a broken person who needs to be saved? A person who needs the approval of others to be ok?

She led me into this year. She led me to teachings that taught me something very different. They taught me I am whole. I am complete. This year had actually taught me I was far stronger than I thought, and that strength came from compassion and courage, not aggression and abuse.

And somehow here I was, in the middle of the night, alive.

I survived 2013.

Maybe now, instead of being burned, I could light the fire myself and make the choice about what I wanted to burn moving forward.

I reach into my pocket to pull out the piece of paper I had tucked so carefully there from the plane and take a moment to survey my words. Yes, this is what I want to release. Standing over my parents' kitchen sink, I take a lighter and click the flame to life, placing it at the corner of the sheet.

Flames erupt from the paper, burning with the rigor of fresh kindle in a bonfire. The kitchen fills with smoke, and before I know it, the smoke alarm is going off and filling the house. I start dousing the fire with water and frantically trying to wave at the smoke with a towel.

My parents come charging to the top of the stairs asking, "Are you ok? Is everything ok?"

Completely embarrassed, I squeak out, "Everything is fine..."

"What are you doing?" my mother asks with incredulity.

"I was just burning some paper. Creating a New Year's ritual."

There is total silence, and my parents head back to bed.

Once I hear their door close, I look down at the soaked grey pieces of paper in the sink and smile.

Then I giggle under my breath, and then I laugh.

I laugh and laugh and laugh.

End of Year Gratitude 2013

Grateful for

- my parents
- friends
- my practice
- Zen
- yoga
- therapy
- meditation
- quiet
- Guatemala
- a chance to speak my shame
- gaining clarity
- ending my affair

Dream Journal Entry
12/31/13

I'm in a large concert, huge venue, like a stadium, performing a theme-like show. I'm not certain of the steps, but it doesn't seem to really matter. As the show goes on, I know fewer and fewer cast members until the end when I know no one on stage. We take a big picture, and I'm happy.

When The Violin

When
The violin
Can forgive the past

It starts singing.

When the violin can stop worrying
About the future

You will become
Such a drunk laughing nuisance

That God
Will then lean down
And start combing you into
His
Hair.

When the violin can forgive
Every wound caused by
Others

The heart starts
Singing.

— Hafiz

THE NUMBER 2

TWO IS THE SMALLEST even number and has many romantic associations around partnership, marriage, and coupling.

In Chinese culture, it is believed to be very auspicious, based on the belief that "good things come in pairs." For wedding ceremonies, there is a tradition to decorate gates and windows with the double happiness symbol, which is two copies side by side of the Chinese symbol that means joy and happiness. In Feng Shui, the double happiness is used as a cure for love, and is a symbol for balance, flow, and symmetry, often placed in the bedroom.

"Bi Yi Shuang Fei" in Chinese means flying wing to wing, pointing to the cultural definition that the number two symbolizes harmony.

The number 2 also symbolizes societal and mental dualities. Many humans prefer a two-valued logic, which puts everything into a category like: me/you, masculine/feminine, yes/no, right/wrong, left/right, friend/foe, good/evil, and so on.

These dualities make up dualism, a perception that whatever we encounter with our senses can be sorted into a contrasting pair. This can create a sense of safety as we navigate our lives but can also create an immense amount of suffering and violence. Every war has been based on the belief of dualism, and the taking of lives, land, and basic human rights. If I'm right and you're wrong, I have the authority to create harm and force you to change or leave. And this journey really begins with how we view ourselves, if we are at war within and not accepting all aspects of ourselves.

It's important to know that just because something comes in a pair doesn't make it dual, or mutually exclusive. The yin-yang symbol might look dualistic, but it is asking us to discover and see something much more powerful in ourselves and in the world. The opposing areas of the symbol represent masculine and feminine energies from which all phenomena take existence. They are part of each other and cannot exist without each other. We are both yin *and* yang. Dualism is really just an illusion we have created in our minds, histories, and bodies.

Buddhism proposes that all things are interdependent and inter-exist, stating nothing is separate. Things are the way they are because everything else is the way it is. All distinctions we make between dualities, or this and that, are arbitrary and exist only in our minds. This doesn't mean that nothing exists, but that nothing exists the way we think it does.

SECTION 3

EPILOGUE

---

or 1+1=2
or 2+2=4

"The curious paradox is that when I accept myself just as I am, then I can change."

– Carl Rogers

"RECLAIM YOUR LIFE IN 2014!" I read one more time.

I've never done this before. I've never signed up for a webinar, and then booked a time to speak to a life coach.

I've never spoken to any kind of coach.

But, oh, how I want to take advantage of how I feel.

This month is feeling very different. I feel possibility. I don't feel like another horrible thing is waiting around the corner, or ready to drop from the sky. I truly feel in my gut that the worst is over. I survived 2013, and now that I have this new year ahead of me, I want it to count.

I want 2014 to truly be a new beginning, but I have NO idea how to do it. I went straight from my parents' home into a married home. I was never single, and now I'm in my late 30s. I have no idea how to create my own life, how to find love again, and I want to learn how.

And I want to use this energy of January to set my new life in motion. I'm in a huge pile of ash from last year. The fire has stopped, and when I look skyward, I see blue. Looking down, I know this is fertile soil, the warmth of the embers calling me forward. It's time to plant some seeds.

My phone rings, and I pick up. I'm nervous as hell but feel a kinship with this coach, and her voice calms me. After introductions and some small talk, she dives in with a question I've been waiting to be asked.

With a strong focus, she asks, "What do you want?"

And pouring out of my mouth comes my deepest vision of my own family and the career I love. I've never spoken this out loud, not to any of my friends, family or therapist. It's ambitious and incredibly tender, my desire to have a loving life partner and children. My desire to feel fearless in my career and on purpose with my work.

I voice my biggest dreams.

I finish, and there is a moment of silence. I can feel myself starting to retreat. Oh God, what was I thinking? Sharing all of this with a stranger? Does it sound like too much? Is she thinking I'm crazy to want all of this?

And then she says, "You know that's possible, right?"

Something shifts. I exhale and lean forward in my apartment in complete relief.

She believes it's possible. I believe it's possible. That's two people.

So I say Yes.

Yes to working with her.

Yes to reclaiming my life.

Yes to my vision.

Yes to dating for the first time in my life.

13 months later, it's time to create something new.

UMBRELLA

ONE MORE SUBWAY STOP TO GO. I check my makeup in my mirror, and everything is freshly applied after Zen service.

He went into action after I sent a text earlier this week saying, "I find it really sexy when a man plans." I've only been to the Brooklyn Botanical Gardens and Art Museum one other time, and never had a guy plan something so special for the first date.

I smile as I recall our phone conversation earlier in the week and how easy it was to talk to him. I'm excited to meet him.

The doors open, and I gather my things, climbing the steps to the street to see a blue-eyed man waiting at the top, holding an umbrella. We hug, and he leads me towards the entrance of the Botanical Gardens. Just after entering, a slight rain begins, and without missing a beat, he opens his umbrella, takes my arm and says, "So, tell me about Zen service."

My breath catches for a moment. I've dated a lot of men who were curious about my Zen practice, and most kept a distance. I knew I wanted a man who had faith in something, but I had given up on finding a man who actually shared my practice. For years, I'd hoped to meet a man at the temple with no luck. I'd hoped to meet a man at my yoga studio with no luck. I had even made a new vision board with two meditation cushions side by side last year, but was really doubting that vision could ever come true.

I exhale and share about the morning of meditation, about how much I love going on Sundays, and how moving the dharma discourse was, and he takes in everything with those big blue eyes, nodding his head and smiling at me. I'm feeling warm underneath my coat.

The rain stops, and we make our way through the garden. He patiently waits as I take photos of the flowers, and conversation is flowing with such ease. We come to a large cluster of cherry blossoms and see a mother and daughter posing. I offer to take their picture, and she then says, "Oh! Would you like me to take one of the two of you?"

I freeze, as I've never taken a picture with a first date before, but he joyfully says, "Yes!"

Feeling slightly awkward and amazed, I fumble with my phone as the mother hands it back to me. I look down at a beautiful photo of a shining, smiling couple. We do look nice together.

We head into the museum, and after checking our coats, I run to the bathroom. When I come out, there he is. Waiting for me. This is a first. I've never had a date do this before, especially not on the first date. How did he know that means so much to me? He puts his arm around me, and we head into the gallery. His arms feel so nice.

We walk through the exhibits, and I feel his arm brush against my back. I feel flirty, feminine and happy. I'm loving talking about each piece and hearing his views in return.

We grab a bite to eat, and he leans over and kisses me on the cheek, saying, "I'm having a really nice time." My heart skips a beat because I realize I am too.

I really am.

On the subway back home, I take out my phone and open my notes app to write down my feelings and needs, a Nonviolent Communication exercise taught to me by my love coach last year. It's been transformative in helping me to clarify if I want to see each man again, so I have done this process for every date I've been on. Nonviolent

Communication has had such an enormous impact on my life, and I'm teaching it to all my clients.

Feelings:

I feel curious, enchanted, fascinated, stimulated, ardent, energetic, enlivened, exuberant, surprised, vibrant, radiant, touched, cheerful, delighted, giddy, merry, confident, up, amazed, renewed.

Needs Met:

Self expression, acceptance, affection, authenticity, closeness, communication, communion, companionship, consideration, intimacy, mutuality, partnership, security, shared reality, support, trust, consciousness, presence, beauty, ease, faith, harmony, hope, order, care, food, touch, adventure, fun, joy, stimulation.

And I realize that so many needs that have not been met by all the other men I have dated over the past three and half years were met by him.

And most of all, I realize I felt relaxed around him.

When I first began dating, I had so many sensations erupt within me that I didn't understand. There was this tension, as if I was jumping out of my body. I thought it was excitement and a sign the relationship was moving forward, until I found myself ghosted, or lied to. I was 38 and dating for the first time, having married at the tender age of 22. I was awkward and lost. I needed some serious help!

So I hired a love coach, and she asked a question that changed the course of my dating and offered me a tool I had never considered. She asked, "How will you feel in your body with your man?"

Through therapy and recognizing how much I had tried to control my ex, I first recognized how it felt in my body when I wanted to change someone. It felt crazy-making, like all my energy was pulsing outside of me in waves. There was also this huge rush of adrenaline.

So, I quickly learned that the opposite of that was relaxation. Much like my meditation practice that had finally given me the ability to see my thoughts and transform how I showed up, I learned that dating was no different.

Turns out I had been VERY anxious, angry, and exhausted for years in my marriage.

And I promised myself after my divorce that I would not marry another man like my ex. So I practiced sitting in front of my dates feeling relaxed. I practiced at home, sitting and imagining feeling relaxed in my body as my life partner held my hand.

And through each disappointment, I kept practicing.

Earlier this year, the ball dropped on Times Square with 2017 glittering through the cold air, and I made a decision that the single most important thing to me this year was finding my life partner. I had spent the last two years building my business, but as my early 40s ticked on, my vision of a family called with deep urgency.

So, I kept practicing. I kept dating.

But I've never had a first date like this. This feels completely different. On every other first date, I had this premonition of what would go wrong. I would feel something that was unavailable, some pain or behavior that was a red flag.

But not today.

Today I just enjoyed myself. I think I have finally begun to accept who I am, to be relaxed within my own body. Perhaps this date came at the right time, and it's not just about how good he feels, but how good I feel regardless.

This feels so different.

What a miracle.

Wedding Vows

A single petal
curled outward from the
vibrantly pink tight bud;
poised, hopeful
she slowly unfurls,
encouraged gently among
May cherry blossoms.
Even with every membrane
alive with karma,
she finally relaxes
in a sky of blue.
In the descent, releasing her clutch
a chain awakens
at the base
opening each petal in turn,
then another,
then another.

Turns out, it was all
connected.
The winter years
so tightly knit,
so deeply felt,
release in the basking glow
of a word I now vow to
make my living practice,
Love.

What is it to love you,
Chuck?
What is it to love myself in your presence?
What is it to love you in

sickness and health?
In conflict and
deep sorrow?
I vow to make this
my living question.

I vow to choose love in
our home.
I vow to choose honesty.
I vow to communicate
when I'm struggling
and scared.
I vow to choose
compassion, even if it
means removing myself
to
breathe and reflect.

I vow to see your heart,
beating in every
human breath,
and honoring your
basic goodness and
masculine presence.

20 years ago I stood
before witnesses
believing I understood
this act.
I honor and love that
woman
whose long sleep brought
me to this day.

Today, I meet her on the
shore
and turn to you whole,
my dear love.

NIKÓL ROGERS

I vow to awaken within
our clasped hands
and joined lives,
from the crickets' song to
the dying leaves.
Unfurled in this sacred
space,
petals open for all to see,

I vow to love you
Charles.

Lights on and Awake.

*Each morning we
are born again.*

*What we do today
is what matters
most.*

– Buddha

ACKNOWLEDGMENTS

FROM THE MOMENT THE BALL dropped in 2014, I knew I would write this book. What I didn't know at the time was how it would end, nor when I would actually write it. Many years passed where I thought I would sit down to transcribe my story, yet another December would then roll by. And in the meantime, I would share this story on my blog, podcasts, and interviews and see people's eyes well with tears, or mouths drop open in disbelief. My readers would respond to my blog with their own moments of devastation. I would hear and read again and again, "Me too." So I knew this story had to be written.

And then, in 2021, in the ongoing chaotic global crisis, I opened my computer and finally started to write.

I found a loving flow, and that it was actually the divine time to put it all into words.

That flow is the result of an enormous amount of support, care, and presence from the people in my life, and especially the people who held my hand and stood beside me during my deepest heartbreak in 2013. I want to take this moment to acknowledge your superhuman love that was a daily inspiration to keep living.

To the friends who listened, gave me keys to your apartments, and responded with such care: Lisa and Chris, Nova Bergeron, Vonnie and Jon Murad, Rachel Grundy, Spence

Ford, Maxime De Toledo, Akshaya Parker, Danny Vaccaro, Matt Leisy, Eileen Ward, and Erica Sweany.

Thank you.

To the teachers and healers who opened my mind, taught me how to turn the light on within, and guided me to start healing my past: Jeff Rubin, Shugen, Claire Moed, Danielle Gregan, Chachi, Victor Colletti, Thomas, Barbara, Michon Peacock, Sabbath McLean, Jacqulyn Buglisi, Tara Brach, Pema Chodron, Thich Nhat Hanh, Sakyong Mipham, Rumi, Hafiz, and Elizabeth Gilbert.

Thank you.

To my family who stood by my side and helped me close out one home and set up a whole new one, standing steadfast in the face of a giant storm: Mom, Dad, Karl, Aunt Bonnie, and Grandma. Grandma, your presence was felt throughout this year, in spirit. I miss you. Mom, thank you for always affirming my writing and encouraging me to do what I love.

Thank you.

From the moment I decided to finally write this book, an incredible creative team emerged to help the birth and bring this experience to you.

Thank you David Wogahn and the whole team at AuthorImprints for all your guidance and advice, especially as a first-time self-publishing author.

Thank you Emily Pollio for your miraculous and sacred designs.

Thank you Caitlin Cannon for continuing to capture my essence with your powerful images. Our collaboration is a flowing well of abundance.

Thank you Nicole Washburn for your probing questions that opened up what this book is all about.

Thank you Caroline Barnhill for your immense care on the manuscript. This story has come alive from your help!

Thank you to my amazing husband, Chuck. You changed my life that day in the Botanical Gardens, and every day, you support me and my writing. Each day with you is a gift. Thank you for seeing me.

And lastly, thank you, Jo-Na Williams. Your unwavering belief in me and this book, in my teaching and my vow has been a pillar of love through all our years of working together. Thank you for being the most incredible coach a woman could ever ask for.

And to you, beautiful reader. Thank you. I bow in deep gratitude to your light, your wholeness, and your beating heart. Thank you for co-creating this journey with me.

ABOUT THE AUTHOR

NIKOL ROGERS is a speaker, writer, and empowerment coach who helps people reclaim their confidence, expand their perfect audience, and bring their fearless vision to life. She has taught her ZenRed Method globally and has helped her clients become more confident versions of themselves and in alignment with their true purpose through her signature course, *Powerful Presence*.

With a 20-year professional performance career that includes kicking eye high as a Rockette, Nikol has stood on countless stages. Her work is greatly influenced by her Zen practice, Qi Gong, Nonviolent Communication, and her decades of experience as an Artist. Nikol teaches that the heart of transformation lies in discovering who you are. It is this journey that unlocks a person's greatest power, and allows you to manifest a life you love.

Her clients and students have published books, sold out events and concerts, created Solo shows, spoken on large stages, and created award-winning businesses that feed and nourish them.

Nikol lives in New Jersey with her life partner and family, and can be found regularly holding binoculars, standing in nature, and fawning over birds.

Meet Nikol at NikolRogers.com, and @Nikol_Rogers. This is her premiere book.

www.ingramcontent.com/pod-product-compliance
Lightning Source LLC
Chambersburg PA
CBHW020230130626
46549CB00005B/1825